MEDITERRANEAN DIET
COOKBOOK FOR BEGINNERS

The Easiest Guide to Eat Healthily and Feel Great Every Day.
How to Improve Your Well-Being with Simple,
Quick and Tasty Mediterranean Dishes

TABLE OF CONTENTS

INTRODUCTION

Mediterranean diet is a specific diet by removing processed foods and is high in saturated fats. It's not necessarily about losing weight, but rather a healthy lifestyle choice. It is about ingesting traditional ingredients consumed by those who live in the Mediterranean basin for a long time. Their diets never changed, so they must do something right. This is a diet rich in fruits, vegetables, and fish. Cooking with olive oil is a fundamental ingredient and ideal replacement for saturated fats and trans fats. Vegetables and fruits grow well in the heat of the Mediterranean continents, so it's not surprising that the locals devour plenty of them. Studies show that the people who live in these regions live longer and better lives. Changing your eating habits to one that is proven to be healthy is a good enough reason to begin.

Many studies that have been done on the Mediterranean diet offered promising results.

- **Heart-healthy diet.** Blood pressure tends to drop significantly on the Mediterranean diet. In other words, it is a natural way to lower the risk of cardiovascular disease. Researchers have found that the Mediterranean diet can reduce your chances of having a stroke and other vascular diseases.

- **Reduced risk of certain cancers.** The Mediterranean diet emphasizes eating plant-based foods and limiting red meat, harmful oils, and processed foods. Hence, these eating habits may provide some protection against malignant diseases. People in Mediterranean countries are overall less likely to die from cancer.

- **Neuroprotective benefits.** The Mediterranean diet may improve brain and cognitive functions in older adults (by 15%). Clinical trials have shown that those who followed this dietary regimen were less likely to develop Alzheimer's, dementia, or insomnia. A new study has found that antioxidants in the Mediterranean diet plan may protect the brain and nerves, cutting the risk of neurological disorders by almost 50%.

- **Weight loss.** The Mediterranean diet is the most natural and most delicious way to lose weight and maintain an ideal body fat percentage. Low-calorie foods such as fruits, vegetables, yogurt, and fish are widely used in the countries that border the Mediterranean Sea. Natural appetite suppressants include beans, legumes, fatty fish, plain dairy products, and high-fiber foods (almost all vegetables, whole-grains, apples, avocado, and chia seeds). Ginger may control the hunger hormone "ghrelin," too. Consuming a small amount of honey has been shown to reduce appetite. And you will become one step closer to dropping severe pounds!

- **Longevity.** The basics of this dietary plan are; however, vital to longevity and healthy living. Other unexpected benefits include reduced risk of developing depression, diabetes management, improved gut health, and better mood.

Vitamins and minerals can be found in plants and animals, but more often than not, fruits and vegetables are much stronger sources. When we consume another animal, we are finishing all the energy and nutrition that the animal has also consumed. On the other hand, plants are first-hand sources of things like calcium, vitamin K, and vitamin C, which our bodies require daily doses of.

So, how can the Mediterranean Diet help you achieve your dreams of a slimmer body?

For a start, the diet requires you to limit processed and sugary foods that are high in calories. Just making this small change will already help you get your calorie intake under control.

Another contributing factor is the healthy fats you'll be eating daily. I know we've been told over and over again that fat makes you fat. To that, I say nonsense, and I have the science to back me! A group of doctors decided to compare weight loss results between low-carb, Mediterranean, and low-fat diets (Shai, 2008). They discovered that those who followed the Mediterranean Diet lost more weight than those on a low-fat diet. Better yet, they maintained their weight loss afterward. The fact of the matter is that fat makes you feel fuller for longer, and when you're sated, gone is the temptation to stick your hand in the cookie jar! Talking about cookies, the healthy fats combined with the protein you'll be consuming while on the Mediterranean Diet will keep your glucose level in check. This means you won't get those nagging cravings for sugary foods. Over the past ten years, many health researchers have forces doctors and dieticians to change the notion of a healthy diet. As a result, discoveries have been made that tell more about the true causes and mechanisms of harmful ailments like cancer, diabetes, and coronary diseases. For this reason, the previous concept of healthy food has been disregarded. Recent research has provided evidence of the benefits of healthy fats in the diet, which led to the development of the Ketogenic diet. The ketogenic diet is a low-carb and high-fat diet that has become a cornerstone for quick weight loss. As a result, the Ketogenic diet is associated with improved blood pressure, blood glucose, and insulin levels.

There is another diet that has become a widely accepted nutritional regime, the Mediterranean diet. Mediterranean diet is known for the prevention of coronary diseases and longevity of life. When the concept for a high-fat Ketogenic diet is combined with the traditional Mediterranean diet's nutrient density and lifestyle factors, a new diet comes into the light—the Ketogenic Mediterranean diet.

The ketogenic Mediterranean diet features 7 to 10% carbohydrates, 55 to 65% fats, 25 to 30% proteins, and 5 to 10% alcohol. It is effortless to merge the Mediterranean diet with the Ketogenic diet. Both diets promote whole eating foods including fresh non-starchy vegetables and fruits, proteins from fish and eggs, cheese, poultry, and meat, high amounts of healthy oils, moderate intake of red wine, and avoiding foods processed or contain sugars, chemicals, or additives. The only difference in this diet is the slight emphasis on different fats and allowing red wine.

Chapter 1:
INTRODUCTION TO MEDITERRANEAN DIET

The Mediterranean Diet is a style of eating that emphasizes whole foods like vegetables, fruits, legumes, nuts, and olive oil. A common misconception is that the Mediterranean Diet consists solely of pasta and pizza. The actual advice given in the diet has more to do with portion control and sticking to unprocessed foods with less added salt, sugar, and fat. As a result of this healthy eating pattern, there are decreased risks for cardiovascular disease, type 2 diabetes, and certain kinds of cancer among other chronic diseases.

Many Mediterranean countries are a part of the Mediterranean Diet Pyramid. The pyramid is split up into different levels. Each level has a certain amount of daily servings based on your calorie intake and your age.

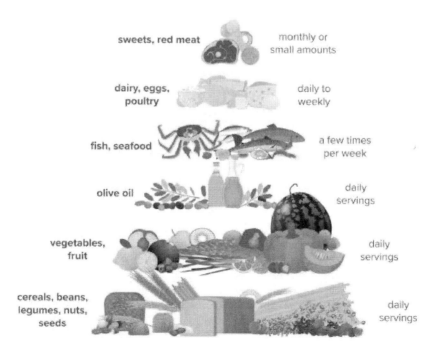

As you can see, the pyramid provides recommendations for different levels of calories per day. The pyramid starts with fruits and vegetables to be consumed daily and it gradually tails off to fewer servings as you get towards the top levels to create a calorie deficit for weight loss or maintenance.

Before jumping into the benefits, it is important to first understand the meaning of the word "Mediterranean." The Mediterranean Sea separates Europe and Africa. Italy, Greece, and Spain are in this region. These three countries symbolize a common genetic and cultural heritage that has been around for thousands of years. When you look at all these countries side by side, there are many similarities with each where they share similar diets, lifestyles, and customs. Through this research, it has been shown that people who live in these areas tend to have lower rates of heart disease, obesity, and other chronic diseases than those in other countries around the world.

What Is the Mediterranean Zone Diet for?Errore. Il segnalibro non è definito.

The goal of this diet is to eat a variety of whole foods and limit the number of processed foods you take in. The Mediterranean Diet is broken down into different categories based on geographical areas and local cultures. Some categories include food staples such as olive oil, legumes, fish, red wine, and nuts that are common throughout the Mediterranean.

Pasta does exist however only in small quantities with a focus on whole-grains rather than refined grains like white rice or flour. Bread can be replaced with a whole-grain roll. Pita bread and pitas are also available but I would avoid them as they are full of added fats and oils. Pasta is typically made out of wheat flour, which means it should not be consumed if you are gluten sensitive. Many vegetables can be used in place of pasta such as zucchini, eggplant, broccoli, etc. Spaghetti is one example of this.

Mediterranean Zone Diet ProgramErrore. Il segnalibro non è definito.

A Mediterranean Zone Diet usually consists of various types of whole-grain breads, whole-grains crackers like pita and pitas with a variety of low-fat spreads such as olive oil and yogurt. Other popular items include vegetables such as tomatoes, peppers, artichokes, and zucchini. The Mediterranean Zone Diet is not only about what you eat but how it is prepared and where it is sourced from. Different types of cuisine are a part of this region. In fact, the word zone not only refers to a geographical region but also to a whole way of nourishing. It all comes down to the cooking style, and the herbs used in the dish. For example, Mediterranean Zone Diet would not contain dishes that heavily use garlic or onion because they have too much sodium. Also, the tomato sauce used could be made from paste instead of canned tomatoes if that is what you like to use.

The Mediterranean Zone Diet has been in practice for thousands of years as it is linked to the Mediterranean culture. It is part of a ton of foods and recipes from the region that is consumed in other countries. Many cultures have adopted this diet over time and adjusted it to suit their needs or added their own twist to it to suit their taste buds better.

This type of diet has health benefits, but there are some downsides to it as well. The main negative aspect is that you have to be careful with portion sizes as well as the amount of food you eat throughout the day, especially if you are following a calorie deficit or goal of weight loss. Overall, the Mediterranean Zone Diet is a great way to eat healthy no matter what your goals are!

The Mediterranean diet is associated with both health and longevity. The diet's proportions of unsaturated fats, including omega-3 fatty acids (fish oil, olive oil) and monounsaturated fats (olive oil), as well as the ratio of macronutrients (low in saturated fats), are linked to a reduction of cardiovascular diseases, an increase in longevity, and better cognitive performance that has been observed throughout the populations that follow this diet.

Studies have also shown that the Mediterranean diet may help prevent cancer and improve longevity.

The Mediterranean diet includes many vegetables, fruits, dairy products, fish, and meat. It is low in red meat (less than 10% of daily intake) and processed meats (less than 3%), red wine (up to three glasses per week), and saturated fat (almost no more than 5% of daily intake). The general guideline is to use olive oil as the primary source of fat. Olive oil can be used for cooking or in salad dressings. Olive oil is better for you because it has a high polyunsaturated to saturated fat ratio. In fact, olive oil is one of the primary reasons that the Mediterranean diet is good for you.

A study of a few hundred volunteers conducted in 2003 suggested that a diet based on the Mediterranean diet would lead to more weight loss and better results in keeping off weight than any other diet. The study also showed that even light changes to food habits can make a difference.

The Mediterranean diet includes lots of fruit, vegetables, and whole-grains. It's rich in omega-3 fatty acids from fish and nuts and rich in antioxidants from fruits and vegetables. It's low in red meat, saturated fat (only small amounts), and sugar (for example most desserts are made with honey).

For many people, the Mediterranean diet is the holy grail of healthy living. This diet is one of the most well-known and popular diets in the world. It's rich in fruits, vegetables, nuts, olive oil, and other foods that fall under this category. But what do these foods really have to say for themselves?

According to research done by The American Journal of Clinical Nutrition in 2007, there was a clear distribution between bad-for-you food groups on one side and good food groups on the other side. The study took into account numerous aspects when looking at different diets, including nutrient density or fruit-to-vegetable ratio, as well as protein quality and dietary fat quality. For example, the study determined that the blood pressure of those on a low-fat diet was lowered to a greater extent than it was for those on a Mediterranean-type diet.

The Mediterranean Diet Components Errore. Il segnalibro non è definito.

- **Fruit:** Fruits are great for making up the majority of your daily intake, but they're also an excellent source of fiber and antioxidants. Studies have shown that eating fruit can decrease risk factors such as heart disease and stroke (Cohn et al., 1992; Peloso et al., 2003). It's also been known to help combat obesity-related metabolic disorders such as diabetes (Tidbinbika et al., 2004).

- **Nuts:** Nuts have been known to be good in the fight against heart disease and diabetes (Lacson et al., 2003). They're also a great source of fiber, which can help lower cholesterol. A study done on young men that were evaluated for the risk factors of heart disease showed that those who ate about 1.5 ounces of nuts or 6ouncesof nuts consumed every day had a much lower risk factor than those without this type of consumption (Erickson et al., 2001).

- **Olive oil:** According to nutritional researchers, olive oil should only be used as a flavoring agent in cooking or as part of the cooking mix within the food. Consuming olive oil for its own nutritional value is too high of a risk for the body to deal with (Spiller & England, 2011).

- **Fish:** Fish consumption has been proven to be an excellent source of Omega-3 fatty acids. These fatty acids are known to help reduce the risk factor of heart disease and stroke. Smaller studies have also shown that eating fish twice a week can reduce the risk factor of death from cardiovascular diseases (He et al., 2009).

- **Poultry:** Poultry is another good source of Omega-3 fatty acids. It's also another food that helps lower the risk factors for cardiovascular diseases, especially if it's eaten in moderation (He et al., 2009).

- **Nuts & seeds:** Nuts and seeds are another great sources of Omega-3 fatty acids. They're also known to protect the heart, lower cholesterol, reduce joint pain and improve the body's ability to use insulin (He et al., 2009).

- **Vegetables:** Vegetables are an excellent source of fiber. For this reason, they're known to lower blood pressure and cholesterol as well as help treat diabetes (He et al., 2009; Lacson et al., 2003).

- **Legumes:** Legumes are a great source of fiber. For this reason, they're known to lower cholesterol and blood pressure as well as help treat diabetes (Lacson et al., 2003).

The Mediterranean Diet Nutritional BreakdownErrore. Il segnalibro non è definito.

As above, the Mediterranean diet is the most well-known and popular dietary regime. This type of diet is largely based on the traditional foods of this region. It shows that different food groups should make up most if not all of a person's daily intake (the exceptions being meat and dairy). The Mediterranean diet contains very little saturated fat, interesting heavy amounts of fiber, and essential amino acids. As a result, it has one of the lowest rates in the storage of body fat in the world. For this reason, many people believe that this is an excellent dietary regime for anybody wishing to lose weight or keep their weight low. The Mediterranean diet is also rich in antioxidants. These antioxidants have been proven to help fight free radicals and prevent cellular damage. Like other diets, the Mediterranean diet is known to be loaded with Omega-3 fats, which increase circulation as well as improve cardiac health. Omega-3's are also known for their ability to calm inflammation within the body and reduce joint pain (Spiller & England, 2011).

History of Mediterranean DietErrore. Il segnalibro non è definito.

The Mediterranean diet is one of the healthiest and most popular diets in the world, and it's actually not a new diet. The term itself was coined by Ancel Keys, an American scientist who studied obesity in the 1950s. His research showed that people living in societies with low-fat diets had lower rates of coronary heart disease than people living with high-fat diets. While this study didn't prove that the Mediterranean Diet caused less cardiovascular disease, it does show us that it's effective for weight loss and healthy cholesterol levels (and is also delicious). The concept of the Mediterranean Diet was also popularized by Dr. Walter Willett at Harvard in the 1980s, but it wasn't until 1992 that he published research on the idea. What are some of the core elements of a Mediterranean diet?

The word "Mediterranean" is also used to describe countries where people eat this way for different reasons. The history of this diet reportedly began in ancient Greece, which is where we get the word "Mediterranean." Today, though, you'll find a lot of people following along with this healthy lifestyle because it helps them to achieve good health and lose weight. But let's have a closer look at the most important aspects of this diet, and learn how you can incorporate them into your daily life. The Mediterranean Diet tends to emphasize lots of fresh, healthy foods such as vegetables, fruits, nuts, and legumes. In addition, fish and poultry are eaten regularly in place of red meat. Because this diet is low in fat and high in nutrients, it tends to be very protein-rich, but also low in refined carbohydrates like sugar (a positive outcome for those looking to lose weight). This leaves us with plenty of energy for the rest of the day without having that sugar crash we have all experienced before. The Mediterranean Diet aims to eat a balance of healthy fats and carbohydrates, particularly fiber. Many people choose to include more fruit and dairy products into their diet as well. The vegetables that are consumed are often freshly prepared so that they're full of nutrients and live enzymes as well. This way, you get all the benefits of a varied diet without taking in any extra calories.

The main focus is on seasonal vegetables such as high-fiber green salads with olive oil for dressing or fresh herbs. Fruits such as melons, berries, and grapes make a regular appearance on this diet. You'll also find high-protein nuts such as almonds or walnuts in addition to traditional seeds like sesame seed or pine nuts.

This type of diet isn't too unusual, as it's similar to the Mediterranean Diet that we've come to know and love over the years. We're still discovering more about this way of eating, but it appears to be beneficial for our health and weight loss goals as well. However, we should be careful not to make this type of diet too complicated or restrictive. We also have to be careful not to go too far with foods that we might find more palatable, like eating a lot of spicy and strong foods. This type of diet has been linked to lower risks of heart disease, diabetes, high blood pressure, and even certain cancers.

As you can see, the Mediterranean Diet is actually quite similar to what it was in ancient Greece but updated. The idea is simple: we should eat a variety of healthy whole foods in moderation, and focus on unrefined carbohydrates for energy instead of refined carbohydrates such as sugar. With this in mind, you'll be enjoying fresh fruit, vegetables, and fish without worrying about all the other food groups that might be missing out on your diet. With the Mediterranean Diet, you can eat filling foods without feeling weighed down or bloated. If you're striving for a healthy weight, this is the diet for you.

So there we have it, the history of how these two diets came to be. The truth is that with the Mediterranean Diet, we're able to achieve our ideal weight and live longer too.

Benefits of Mediterranean DietErrore. Il segnalibro non è definito.

There is an endless list of benefits that come from eating a Mediterranean-style diet. Some of these benefits include improved weight loss, reduced risk of heart disease, improved skin health, and reduced body fat. Here are some other surprising benefits that you may not have known about:

1. **It can help you reverse diabetes:** This type of diet is high in legumes, vegetables, and fruit. The study showed that those who followed a Mediterranean-style diet had an impressive reversal rate compared to those who continued with their existing lifestyle.

2. **It can slow down or prevent age-related cognitive decline:** People who eat healthy foods such as fruits, vegetables, grains, and fish had much lower rates of Alzheimer's disease than those who consumed higher levels of sodium. This is because high sodium levels in your diet increase the storage of fat in your blood which can lead to Alzheimer's disease.

3. **It can help you live longer.**

4. **It can help you sleep better.**

5. **It can increase your longevity:** The Mediterranean-style diet included fruits, vegetables, legumes, and fish. They also had less tobacco consumption and higher levels of physical activity.

6. **It can reduce your cancer risk.**

7. **It can help you better manage your weight.**

8. **It can help you keep your brain healthy.**

9. **It will reduce your risk of Type 2 diabetes and metabolic syndrome.**

10. **It can help you lose weight.**

It's been debated as to whether the Mediterranean diet is good for you or not. Recent studies, which clearly showed that the diet was beneficial for health, have fueled this debate and now more and more people are beginning to use Mediterranean diet diets. It's probably worth knowing what the Mediterranean Diet lifestyle is about if you're planning on trying it out yourself!

The term "Mediterranean" refers to the regions in which Crete, Italy, Spain, and Portugal reside; these countries share a range of commonalities as they find themselves situated along the same latitude line. Basically, because of this unique setting, they have developed a healthy lifestyle that can be characterized as "relaxed." Essentially, the Mediterranean Diet lifestyle contrasts with a lot of the modern diets today because it is comprised of natural and unprocessed foods.

The Mediterranean diet that is popular today actually has its roots in the early 20th century when Ancel Keys, an American scientist, began observing a particular region in Italy. The Lebanese and Syrian communities residing in this area were the ones whose diet was studied, and over time he discovered that this was indeed a healthier group. This revelation called for further research, which led to more studies getting carried out all over Greece, Spain, Italy, etc.

Back then, there wasn't much of a concept of the Mediterranean Diet in the West since there hadn't been any studies performed on the matter. However, since then several studies have been conducted, and it was discovered that people that live in these regions can see great benefits in regards to health. Research has shown that the Mediterranean Diet lifestyle is associated with better digestive health (lower risk of heart disease, cancer, and diabetes), weight loss, increased energy as well as a lower risk of developing Alzheimer's disease. Over time, this diet has become increasingly popular, and it is now commonly followed in the West. The diet basically allows for a wide range of foods, including whole-grains, legumes as well as vegetables. Fruits and nuts are also part of this diet, although alcohol is not allowed (at least not in large amounts).

The Mediterranean Diet lifestyle isn't just about eating healthier; it's about taking pleasure in healthy activities such as socializing or exercising.

Errore. Il segnalibro non è definito.

The Main Ingredients Used in the DietErrore. Il segnalibro non è definito.

Use this basic list whenever you shop for groceries. Ensure that you stock your pantry with all these ingredients and get rid of any other items that are not suitable for your diet.

Your shopping list must include:

- Veggies like arugula, asparagus artichokes, beets, carrots cauliflower, chicory fennel, cucumber, eggplant, garlic, green beans, kale, lettuce, onions peppers, potatoes, pumpkin, spinach tomatoes, and zucchini.

- Fruits like grapes, oranges, apples, pears, prunes, and nectarines.

- Berries like blueberries, strawberries, and raspberries.

- Fresh veggies

- Grains like whole-grain pasta, and whole-grain bread.

- Legumes like beans, lentils, chickpeas, and peas.

- Nuts like walnuts, cashews, and almonds.

- Seeds like pumpkin seeds and sunflower seeds.

- Condiments like turmeric, cinnamon, salt, and pepper.

- Shrimp and shellfish.

- Fish like mackerel, trout, tuna, salmon, and sardines.

- Cheese.

- Yogurt and Greek yogurt.

- Potatoes and sweet potatoes.

- Chicken.

- Eggs.

- Olives.

- Olive oil and avocado oil.

Chapter 2:
BREAKFAST RECIPES

Italian Breakfast Sausage with Baby Potatoes and Vegetables Errore. Il segnalibro non è definito.Errore. Il segnalibro non è definito.

Preparation time: 15 minutes.
Level: Average.
Cooking time: 30 minutes.
Servings: 4
INGREDIENTS:

- 1 pound sweet Italian sausage links, sliced on the bias (diagonal)
- 2 cups baby potatoes, halved
- 2 cups broccoli florets
- 1 cup onions cut into 1-inch chunks
- 2 cups small mushrooms, half or quarter the large ones for uniform size
- 1 cup baby carrots
- 2 tablespoons olive oil
- 1/2 teaspoon garlic powder
- 1/2 teaspoon Italian seasoning
- 1 teaspoon salt
- 1/2 teaspoons pepper

DIRECTIONS:

1. Preheat the oven to 400°F. In a large bowl, add the baby potatoes, broccoli florets, onions, small mushrooms, and baby carrots.
2. Add in the olive oil, salt, pepper, garlic powder, and Italian seasoning and toss to coat evenly. Spread the vegetables onto a sheet pan in one even layer.
3. Arrange the sausage slices on the pan over the vegetables. Bake for 30 minutes—make sure to sake halfway through to prevent sticking. Allow cooling.
4. Distribute the Italian sausages and vegetables among the containers and store them in the fridge for 2–3 days.

NUTRITION: Calories: 321 Fat: 16g Carbs: 23g Protein: 22g

Cauliflower Fritters with Hummus

Preparation time: 15 minutes.
Level: Easy.
Cooking time: 15 minutes.
Servings: 4
INGREDIENTS:

- 2 (15 oz) cans chickpeas, divided
- 2 1/2 tablespoons olive oil, divided, plus more for frying
- 1 cup onion, chopped, about 1/2 a small onion
- 2 tablespoons garlic, minced
- 2 cups cauliflower, cut into small pieces, about 1/2 a large head
- 1/2 teaspoons salt
- Black pepper to taste

Topping:

- Hummus of choice
- Green onion, diced

DIRECTIONS:

1. Preheat the oven to 400°F. Rinse and drain 1 can of the chickpeas, place them on a paper towel to dry off well.
2. Then place the chickpeas into a large bowl, removing the loose skins that come off, and toss with 1 tablespoon of olive oil, spread the chickpeas onto a large pan, and sprinkle with salt and pepper.
3. Bake for 20 minutes, then stir and then bake an additional 5–10 minutes until very crispy.
4. Once the chickpeas are roasted, transfer them to a large food processor and process them until broken down and crumble. Don't over-process them and turn them into flour, as you need to have some texture. Place the mixture into a small bowl, set aside.
5. In a large pan over medium-high heat, add the remaining 1(1/2) tablespoon of olive oil. Once heated, add in the onion and garlic, cook until lightly golden brown, about 2 minutes.
6. Then add in the chopped cauliflower, cook for an additional 2 minutes, until the cauliflower is golden.
7. Turn the heat down to low and cover the pan, cook until the cauliflower is fork-tender and the onions are golden brown and caramelized, stirring often about 3–5 minutes.
8. Transfer the cauliflower mixture to the food processor, drain and rinse the remaining can of chickpeas and add them into the food processor, along with the salt and a pinch of pepper.
9. Blend until smooth, and the mixture starts to ball, stop to scrape down the sides as needed
10. Transfer the cauliflower mixture into a large bowl and add in 1/2 cup of the roasted chickpea crumbs, stir until well combined.
11. In a large bowl over medium heat, add in enough oil to cover the bottom of a large pan. Working in batches, cook the patties until golden brown, about 2–3 minutes, flip and cook again. Serve.

NUTRITION: Calories: 333 Carbohydrates: 45g Fat: 13g Protein: 14g

Overnight Berry Chia Oats

Preparation time: 15 minutes.
Level: Easy.
Cooking time: 5 minutes.
Servings: 4
INGREDIENTS:

- 1/2 cup Quaker oats rolled oats
- 1/4 cup chia seeds
- 1 cup milk or water
- Pinch of salt and cinnamon
- Maple syrup, or a different sweetener, to taste
- 1 cup frozen berries of choice or smoothie leftovers

Toppings:

- Yogurt
- Berries

DIRECTIONS:

1. In a jar with a lid, add the oats, seeds, milk, salt, and cinnamon, refrigerate overnight. On serving day, puree the berries in a blender.
2. Stir the oats, add in the berry puree, and top with yogurt and more berries, nuts, honey, or garnish of your choice. Enjoy!

NUTRITION: Calories: 405 Carbs: 65g Fat: 11g Protein: 17g

Raspberry Vanilla Smoothie

Preparation time: 5 minutes.
Level: Easy.
Cooking time: 5 minutes.
Servings: 4
INGREDIENTS:

- 1 cup frozen raspberries
- 6 ounces container of vanilla Greek yogurt
- ½ cup of unsweetened vanilla almond milk

DIRECTIONS:

1. Take all of your ingredients and place them in a blender. Process until smooth and liquified.

NUTRITION: Calories: 155 Protein: 7g Fat: 2g Carbohydrates: 30g

Blueberry Banana Protein Smoothie

Preparation time: 5 minutes.
Level: Easy.
Cooking time: 5 minutes.
Servings: 4
INGREDIENTS:

- ½ cup frozen and unsweetened blueberries
- ½ banana slices up
- ¾ cup plain nonfat Greek yogurt
- ¾ cup unsweetened vanilla almond milk
- 2 cups of ice cubes

DIRECTIONS:

1. Add all the ingredients into a blender. Blend until smooth.

NUTRITION: Calories: 230 Protein: 19.1g Fat: 2.6g Carbohydrates: 32.9g

Chocolate Banana Smoothie

Preparation time: 5 minutes.
Level: Easy.
Cooking time: 0 minutes.
Servings: 4

INGREDIENTS:

- 2 bananas, peeled
- 1 cup unsweetened almond milk or skim milk
- 1 cup crushed ice
- 3 tablespoons unsweetened cocoa powder
- 3 tablespoons honey

DIRECTIONS:

1. In a blender, combine the bananas, almond milk, ice, cocoa powder, and honey. Blend until smooth.

NUTRITION: Calories: 219 Protein: 2g Carbohydrates: 57g Fat: 2g

Moroccan Avocado Smoothie

Preparation time: 5 minutes.
Level: Easy.
Cooking time: 0 minutes.
Servings: 4
INGREDIENTS:

- 1 ripe avocado, peeled and pitted
- 1 overripe banana
- 1 cup almond milk, unsweetened
- 1 cup of ice

DIRECTIONS:

1. Place the avocado, banana, milk, and ice into your blender. Blend until smooth with no pieces of avocado remaining.

NUTRITION: Calories: 100 Protein: 1g Fat: 6g Carbohydrates: 11g

Greek Yogurt with Fresh Berries, Honey and Nuts

Preparation time: 5 minutes.
Level: Easy.
Cooking time: 0 minutes.
Servings: 4
INGREDIENTS:

- 6 ounces nonfat plain Greek yogurt
- 1/2 cup fresh berries of your choice
- 0.25 ounces crushed walnuts
- 1 tablespoon honey

DIRECTIONS:

1. In a jar with a lid, add the yogurt. Top with berries and a drizzle of honey. Top with the lid and store in the fridge for 2–3 days.

NUTRITION: Calories: 250 Carbs: 35g Fat: 4g Protein: 19g

Greek Beans Tortillas

Preparation time: 5 minutes.
Level: Average.
Cooking time: 20 minutes.
Servings: 4
INGREDIENTS:

- 1 red onion, chopped
- 2 garlic cloves, minced
- 1 tablespoon olive oil
- 1 green bell pepper, sliced
- 3 cups canned pinto beans, drained and rinsed
- 2 red chili peppers, chopped
- 4 tablespoon parsley, chopped
- 1 teaspoon cumin, ground
- A pinch of salt and black pepper
- 4 whole-wheat Greek tortillas
- 1 cup cheddar cheese, shredded

DIRECTIONS:

1. Heat up a pan with the oil over medium heat, add the onion and sauté for 5 minutes.
2. Add the rest of the ingredients except the tortillas and the cheese, stir and cook for 15 minutes.
3. Divide the beans mix on each Greek tortilla, also divide the cheese, roll the tortillas and serve for breakfast.

NUTRITION: Calories: 673 Fat: 14.9g Fiber: 23.7g Carbs: 75.4g Protein: 39g

Bacon, Spinach and Tomato Sandwich

Preparation time: 5 minutes.
Level: Easy.
Cooking time: 0 minutes.
Servings: 4
INGREDIENTS:

- 2 whole-wheat bread slices, toasted
- 1 tablespoon Dijon mustard
- 3 bacon slices
- Salt and black pepper to taste
- 2 tomato slices
- ¼ cup baby spinach

DIRECTIONS:

1. Spread the mustard on each bread slice, divide the bacon and the rest of the ingredients on one slice, top with the other one, cut in half, and serve for breakfast.

NUTRITION: Calories: 246 Fat: 11.2g Fiber: 4.5g Carbs: 17.5g Protein: 8.3g

Coriander Mushroom Salad

Preparation time: 5 minutes.
Level: Easy.
Cooking time: 7 minutes.
Servings: 4
INGREDIENTS:

- ½ pounds white mushrooms, sliced
- 1 tablespoon olive oil
- 3 garlic cloves, minced
- Salt and black pepper to taste
- 1 tomato, diced
- 1 avocado, peeled, pitted, and cubed
- 3 tablespoons lime juice
- ½ cup chicken stock
- 2 tablespoons coriander, chopped

DIRECTIONS:

1. Heat up a pan with the oil over medium heat, add the mushrooms and sauté them for 4 minutes.
2. Add the rest of the ingredients, toss, cook for 3–4 minutes more, divide into bowls and serve for breakfast.

NUTRITION: Calories: 320 Fat: 11.2g Fiber: 8.3g Carbohydrates: 4.2g Protein: 10g

Cinnamon Apple and Lentils Porridge

Preparation time: 5 minutes.
Level: Easy.
Cooking time: 10 minutes.
Servings: 4
INGREDIENTS:

- ½ cup walnuts, chopped
- 2 green apples, cored, peeled, and cubed
- 3 tablespoons maple syrup
- 3 cups almond milk
- ½ cup red lentils
- ½ teaspoon cinnamon powder
- ½ cup cranberries, dried
- 1 teaspoon vanilla extract

DIRECTIONS:

1. Put the milk in a pot, heat it up over medium heat, add the walnuts, apples, maple syrup, and the rest of the ingredients, toss, simmer for 10 minutes, divide into bowls and serve.

NUTRITION: Calories: 150 Fat: 2g Fiber: 1g Carbs: 3g Protein: 5g

Seeds and Lentils Oats

Preparation time: 10 minutes.
Level: Average.
Cooking time: 50 minutes.
Servings: 4
INGREDIENTS:

- ½ cup red lentils
- ¼ cup pumpkin seeds, toasted
- 2 teaspoons olive oil
- ¼ cup rolled oats
- ¼ cup coconut flesh, shredded
- 1 tablespoon honey
- 1 tablespoon orange zest, grated
- 1 cup Greek yogurt
- 1 cup blackberries

DIRECTIONS:

1. Spread the lentils on a baking sheet lined with parchment paper, introduce them to the oven, and roast at 370°F for 30 minutes.
2. Add the rest of the ingredients except the yogurt and the berries, toss and bake at 370°F for 20 minutes more.
3. Transfer this to a bowl, add the rest of the ingredients, toss, divide into smaller bowls and serve for breakfast.

NUTRITION: Calories: 204 Fat: 7.1g Fiber 10.4g Carbs: 27.6g Protein: 9.5g

Orzo and Veggie Bowls

Preparation time: 10 minutes.
Level: Easy.
Cooking time: 0 minutes.
Servings: 4
INGREDIENTS:

- 2(½) cups whole-wheat orzo, cooked
- 14 ounces canned cannellini beans, drained and rinsed
- 1 yellow bell pepper, cubed
- 1 green bell pepper, cubed
- A pinch of salt and black pepper
- 3 tomatoes, cubed
- 1 red onion, chopped
- 1 cup mint, chopped
- 2 cups feta cheese, crumbled
- 2 tablespoons olive oil
- ¼ cup lemon juice
- 1 tablespoon lemon zest, grated
- 1 cucumber, cubed
- 1(¼) cup kalamata olives, pitted and sliced
- 3 garlic cloves, minced

DIRECTIONS:

1. In a salad bowl, combine the orzo with the beans, bell peppers, and the rest of the ingredients, toss, divide the mix between plates and serve for breakfast.

NUTRITION: Calories: 411 Fat: 17g Fiber: 13g Carbs: 51g Protein: 14g

Lemon Peas Quinoa Mix

Preparation time: 10 minutes.
Level: Average.
Cooking time: 20 minutes.
Servings: 4
INGREDIENTS:

- 1(½) cups quinoa, rinsed
- 1-pound asparagus, steamed and chopped
- 3 cups water
- 2 tablespoons parsley, chopped
- 2 tablespoons lemon juice
- 1 teaspoon lemon zest, grated
- ½ pound sugar snap peas, steamed
- ½ pound green beans, trimmed and halved
- A pinch of salt and black pepper
- 3 tablespoons pumpkin seeds
- 1 cup cherry tomatoes, halved
- 2 tablespoons olive oil

DIRECTIONS:

1. Put the water in a pot, bring to a boil over medium heat, add the quinoa, stir and simmer for 20 minutes.
2. Stir the quinoa, add the parsley, lemon juice, and the rest of the ingredients, toss, divide between plates and serve for breakfast.

NUTRITION: Calories: 417 Fat: 15g Fiber: 9g Carbs: 58g Protein: 16g

Walnuts Yogurt Mix

Preparation time: 10 minutes.
Level: Easy.
Cooking time: 0 minutes.
Servings: 4
INGREDIENTS:
- 2(½) cups Greek yogurt
- 1(½) cups walnuts, chopped
- 1 teaspoon vanilla extract
- ¾ cup honey
- 2 teaspoons cinnamon powder

DIRECTIONS:
1. In a bowl, combine the yogurt with the walnuts and the rest of the ingredients, toss, divide into smaller bowls and keep in the fridge for 10 minutes before serving for breakfast.

NUTRITION: Calories: 388 Fat: 24.6g Fiber: 2.9g Carbs: 39.1g Protein: 10.2g

Stuffed Pita Breads

Preparation time: 5 minutes.
Level: Easy.
Cooking time: 15 minutes.
Servings: 4
INGREDIENTS:

- 1(½) tablespoon olive oil
- 1 tomato, cubed
- 1 garlic clove, minced
- 1 red onion, chopped
- ¼ cup parsley, chopped
- 15 ounces canned fava beans, drained and rinsed
- ¼ cup lemon juice
- Salt and black pepper to taste
- 4 whole-wheat pita bread pockets

DIRECTIONS:

1. Heat up a pan with the oil over medium heat, add the onion, stir, and sauté for 5 minutes.
2. Add the rest of the ingredients, stir and cook for 10 minutes more
3. Stuff the pita pockets with this mix and serve for breakfast.

NUTRITION: Calories: 382 Fat: 1.8g Fiber: 27.6g Carbs: 66g Protein: 28.5g

Farro Salad

Preparation time: 5 minutes.
Level: Easy.
Cooking time: 4 minutes.
Servings: 4
INGREDIENTS:

- 1 tablespoon olive oil
- A pinch of salt and black pepper
- 1 bunch baby spinach, chopped
- 1 avocado, pitted, peeled, and chopped
- 1 garlic clove, minced
- 2 cups farro, already cooked
- ½ cup cherry tomatoes, cubed

DIRECTIONS:

1. Heat up a pan with the oil over medium heat, add the spinach, and the rest of the ingredients, toss, cook for 4 minutes, divide into bowls and serve.

NUTRITION: Calories: 157 Fat: 13.7g Fiber: 5.5g Carbs: 8.6g Protein: 3.6g

Cranberry and Dates Squares

Preparation time: 30 minutes.
Level: Easy.
Cooking time: 0 minutes.
Servings: 4
INGREDIENTS:

- 12 dates, pitted and chopped
- 1 teaspoon vanilla extract
- ¼ cup honey
- ½ cup rolled oats
- ¾ cup cranberries, dried
- ¼ cup almond avocado oil, melted
- 1 cup walnuts, roasted and chopped
- ¼ cup pumpkin seeds

DIRECTIONS:

1. In a bowl, mix the dates with the vanilla, honey, and the rest of the ingredients, stir well and press everything on a baking sheet lined with parchment paper.
2. Keep in the freezer for 30 minutes, cut into 10 squares and serve for breakfast.

NUTRITION: Calories: 263 Fat: 13.4g Fiber: 4.7g Carbs: 14.3g Protein: 3.5g

Chapter 3:
PASTA DISHES

Creamy Pumpkin Pasta

Preparation time: 15 minutes.
Level: Average.
Cooking time: 30 minutes.
Servings: 4
INGREDIENTS:

- 1-pound whole-grain linguine
- 1 tablespoon olive oil
- 3 garlic cloves, peeled and minced
- 2 tablespoons chopped fresh sage
- 1(½) cups pumpkin purée
- 1 cup unsalted vegetable stock
- ½ cup low-fat evaporated milk
- ¾ teaspoon kosher or sea salt
- ½ teaspoon ground black pepper
- ½ teaspoon ground nutmeg
- ¼ teaspoon ground cayenne pepper
- ½ cup freshly grated Parmesan cheese, divided

DIRECTIONS:

1. Cook the whole-grain linguine in a large pot of boiled water. Reserve ½ cup of pasta water and drain the rest. Set the pasta aside.
2. Warm-up olive oil over medium heat in a large skillet. Add the garlic and sage and sauté for 1 to 2 minutes until soft and fragrant. Whisk in the pumpkin purée, stock, milk, and reserved pasta water and simmer for 4 to 5 minutes, until thickened.
3. Whisk in the salt, black pepper, nutmeg, and cayenne pepper, and half of the Parmesan cheese. Stir in the cooked whole-grain linguine. Evenly divide the pasta among 6 bowls and top with the remaining Parmesan cheese.

NUTRITION: Calories: 381 Fat: 8g Sodium: 175mg Carbohydrate: 63g Protein: 15g

Vegetable Pasta

Preparation time: 15 minutes.
Level: Easy.
Cooking time: 15 minutes.
Servings: 4
INGREDIENTS:

- 1 kilogram of thin zucchini
- 20 grams of fresh ginger
- 350 grams smoked tofu
- 1 lime
- 2 cloves of garlic
- 2 tablespoons sunflower oil
- 2 tablespoons of sesame seeds
- Pinch of salt and pepper
- 4 tablespoons fried onions

DIRECTIONS:

1. Wash and clean the zucchini and, using a julienne cutter, cut the pulp around the kernel into long thin strips (noodles). Ginger peel and finely chops. Crumble tofu. Halve lime squeeze juice. Peel and chop garlic.
2. Warm-up 1 tablespoon of oil in a large pan and fry the tofu for about 5 minutes. After about 3 minutes, add ginger, garlic, and sesame. Season with soy sauce. Remove from the pan and keep warm.
3. Wipe out the pan, then warm 2 tablespoons of oil in it. Stir-fry zucchini strips for about 4 minutes while turning. Season with salt, pepper, and lime juice. Arrange pasta and tofu. Sprinkle with fried onions.

NUTRITION: Calories: 262 Fat: 17.7g Protein: 15.4g Sodium: 62mg Carbohydrate: 17.1g

Aromatic Whole-Grain Spaghetti

Preparation time: 15 minutes.
Level: Easy.
Cooking time: 10 minutes.
Servings: 4
INGREDIENTS:

- 1 teaspoon dried basil
- ¼ cup of soy milk
- 6ounceswhole-grain spaghetti
- 2 cups of water
- 1 teaspoon ground nutmeg

DIRECTIONS:

1. Bring the water to boil, add spaghetti, and cook them for 8–10 minutes. Meanwhile, bring the soy milk to boil. Drain the cooked spaghetti and mix them up with soy milk, ground nutmeg, and dried basil. Stir the meal well.

NUTRITION: Calories. 128 Protein: 5.6g Carbohydrates: 25g Fat: 1.4g Sodium: 25mg

Chapter 4:
RICE DISHES

Wild Rice, Celery, and Cauliflower Pilaf

Preparation time: 15 minutes.
Level: Difficult.
Cooking time: 45 minutes.
Servings: 4
INGREDIENTS:
- 1 tablespoon olive oil, plus more for greasing the baking dish
- 1 cup wild rice
- 2 cups low-sodium chicken broth
- 1 sweet onion, chopped
- 2 stalks celery, chopped
- 1 teaspoon minced garlic
- 2 carrots, peeled, halved lengthwise, and sliced
- ½ cauliflower head, cut into small florets
- 1 teaspoon chopped fresh thyme
- Sea salt to taste

DIRECTIONS:
1. Preheat the oven to 350°f (180°c). Line a baking sheet with parchment paper and grease with olive oil.
2. Put the wild rice in a saucepan, then pour in the chicken broth. Bring to a boil. Reduce the heat to low and simmer for 30 minutes or until the rice is plump.
3. Meanwhile, heat the remaining olive oil in an oven-proof skillet over medium-high heat until shimmering.
4. Add the onion, celery, and garlic to the skillet and sauté for 3 minutes or until the onion is translucent.
5. Add the carrots and cauliflower to the skillet and sauté for 5 minutes. Turn off the heat and set it aside.
6. Pour the cooked rice into the skillet with the vegetables. Sprinkle with thyme and salt. Set the skillet in the preheated oven and bake for 15 minutes or until the vegetables are soft. Serve immediately.

NUTRITION: Calories: 214 Fat: 3.9g Protein: 7.2g Carbs: 37.9g

Papaya, Jicama, and Peas Rice Bowl

Preparation time: 15 minutes.
Level: Difficult.
Cooking time: 45 minutes.
Servings: 4
INGREDIENTS:
Sauce:

- Juice of ¼ lemon
- 2 teaspoons chopped fresh basil
- 1 tablespoon raw honey
- 1 tablespoon extra-virgin olive oil
- Sea salt, to taste

Rice:

- 1(½) cups wild rice
- 2 papayas, peeled, seeded, and diced
- 1 jicama, peeled and shredded
- 1 cup snow peas, julienned
- 2 cups shredded cabbage
- 1 scallion, white and green parts, chopped

DIRECTIONS:

1. Combine the ingredients for the sauce in a bowl. Stir to mix well. Set aside until ready to use. Pour the wild rice in a saucepan, then pour in enough water to cover. Bring to a boil.
2. Reduce the heat to low, then simmer for 45 minutes or until the wild rice is soft and plump. Drain and transfer to a large serving bowl.
3. Top the rice with papayas, jicama, peas, cabbage, and scallion. Pour the sauce over and stir to mix well before serving.

NUTRITION: Calories: 446 Fat: 7.9g Protein: 13.1g Carbs: 85.8g

Mediterranean Lentils and Rice

Preparation time: 5 minutes
Level: Easy
Cooking time: 25 minutes
Servings: 4
INGREDIENTS:

- 2(¼) cups low-sodium or no-salt-added vegetable broth
- ½ cup uncooked brown or green lentils
- ½ cup uncooked instant brown rice
- ½ cup diced carrots (about 1 carrot)
- ½ cup diced celery (about 1 stalk)
- 1 (2.25-ounce) can sliced olives, drained (about ½ cup)
- ¼ cup diced red onion (about 1/8 onion)
- ¼ cup chopped fresh curly-leaf parsley
- 1 (½) tablespoons extra-virgin olive oil
- 1 tablespoon freshly squeezed lemon juice (from about ½ small lemon)
- 1 garlic clove, minced (about ½ teaspoon)
- ¼ teaspoon kosher or sea salt
- ¼ teaspoon freshly ground black pepper

DIRECTIONS:

1. In a medium saucepan over high heat, bring the broth and lentils to a boil, cover, and lower the heat to medium-low. Cook for 8 minutes.
2. Raise the heat to medium, and stir in the rice. Cover the pot and cook the mixture for 15 minutes, or until the liquid is absorbed. Remove the pot from the heat and let it sit, covered, for 1 minute, then stir.
3. While the lentils and rice are cooking, mix together the carrots, celery, olives, onion, and parsley in a large serving bowl.
4. In a small bowl, whisk together the oil, lemon juice, garlic, salt, and pepper. Set aside. When the lentils and rice are cooked, add them to the serving bowl.
5. Pour the dressing on top, and mix everything together. Serve warm or cold, or store in a sealed container in the refrigerator for up to 7 days.

NUTRITION: Calories: 230 Fat: 8g Carbohydrates: 34g Protein: 8g

Brown Rice Pilaf with Golden Raisins

Preparation time: 5 minutes.
Level: Easy.
Cooking time: 15 minutes.
Servings: 4
INGREDIENTS:

- 1 tablespoon extra-virgin olive oil
- 1 cup chopped onion (about ½ medium onion)
- ½ cup shredded carrot (about 1 medium carrot)
- 1 teaspoon ground cumin
- ½ teaspoon ground cinnamon
- 2 cups instant brown rice
- 1¾ cups 100% orange juice
- ¼ cup water
- 1 cup golden raisins
- ½ cup shelled pistachios
- Chopped fresh chives (optional)

DIRECTIONS:

1. In a medium saucepan over medium-high heat, heat the oil. Add the onion and cook for 5 minutes, stirring frequently.
2. Add the carrot, cumin, and cinnamon, and cook for 1 minute, stirring frequently. Stir in the rice, orange juice, and water.
3. Bring to a boil, cover, then lower the heat to medium-low. Simmer for 7 minutes, or until the rice is cooked through and the liquid is absorbed. Stir in the raisins, pistachios, and chives (if using) and serve.

NUTRITION: Calories: 320 Fat: 7g Carbohydrates: 61g Protein: 6g

Cherry, Apricot, and Pecan Brown Rice Bowl

Preparation time: 15 minutes.
Level: Difficult.
Cooking time: 1 hour & 1 minute.
Servings: 4
INGREDIENTS:

- 2 tablespoons olive oil
- 2 green onions, sliced
- ½ cup brown rice
- 1 cup low-sodium chicken stock
- 2 tablespoons dried cherries
- 4 dried apricots, chopped
- 2 tablespoons pecans, toasted and chopped
- Sea salt and freshly ground pepper, to taste

DIRECTIONS:

1. Heat the olive oil in a medium saucepan over medium-high heat until shimmering. Add the green onions and sauté for 1 minute or until fragrant.
2. Add the rice. Stir to mix well, then pour in the chicken stock. Bring to a boil. Reduce the heat to low. Cover and simmer for 50 minutes or until the brown rice is soft.
3. Add the cherries, apricots, and pecans, and simmer for 10 more minutes or until the fruits are tender.
4. Pour them in a large serving bowl. Fluff with a fork. Sprinkle with sea salt and freshly ground pepper. Serve immediately.

NUTRITION: Calories: 451 Fat: 25.9g Protein: 8.2g Carbs: 50.4g

Hearty Barley Risotto

Preparation time: 15 minutes.
Level: Difficult.
Cooking time: 60 minutes.
Servings: 4
INGREDIENTS:

- 1 carrot, peeled and chopped fine
- 1 cup dry white wine
- 1 onion, chopped fine
- 1 teaspoon minced fresh thyme or ¼ teaspoon dried
- 1(½) cups pearl barley
- 2 ounces parmesan cheese, grated (1 cup)
- 2 tablespoons extra-virgin olive oil
- 4 cups chicken or vegetable broth
- 4 cups water
- Salt and pepper to taste

DIRECTIONS:

1. Bring broth and water to simmer in a moderate-sized saucepan. Decrease the heat to low and cover to keep warm.
2. Heat 1 tablespoon oil in a Dutch oven on moderate heat until it starts to shimmer. Put in onion and carrot and cook till they become tender for 5 to 7 minutes.
3. Put in barley and cook, stirring frequently, until lightly toasted and aromatic about 4 minutes. Put in wine and cook, stirring often, until fully absorbed, approximately two minutes.
4. Mix in 3 cups warm broth and thyme, bring to simmer, and cook stirring intermittently, until liquid is absorbed and bottom of the pot is dry, 22 to 25 minutes.
5. Mix in 2 cups warm broth, bring to simmer, and cook stirring intermittently until liquid is absorbed and bottom of the pot is dry, fifteen to twenty minutes.
6. Carry on cooking risotto, stirring frequently and adding warm broth as required to stop the pot bottom from becoming dry, until barley is cooked through, 15 to 20 minutes.
7. Remove from the heat, adjust consistency with the remaining warm broth as required. Mix in Parmesan and residual 1 tablespoon oil and sprinkle with salt and pepper to taste. Serve.

NUTRITION: Calories: 222 Carbs: 33g Fat: 5g Protein: 6g

Rice and Blueberry Stuffed Sweet Potatoes

Preparation time: 15 minutes.
Level: Average.
Cooking time: 20 minutes.
Servings: 4
INGREDIENTS:

- 2 cups cooked wild rice
- ½ cup dried blueberries
- ½ cup chopped hazelnuts
- ½ cup shredded Swiss chard
- 1 teaspoon chopped fresh thyme
- 1 scallion, white and green parts, peeled and thinly sliced
- Sea salt and freshly ground black pepper to taste
- 4 sweet potatoes, baked in the skin until tender

DIRECTIONS:

1. Preheat the oven to 400°F (205°C). Combine all the ingredients, except for the sweet potatoes, in a large bowl. Stir to mix well.
2. Cut the top third of the sweet potato off-length wire, then scoop most of the sweet potato flesh out. Fill the potato with the wild rice mixture, then set the sweet potato on a greased baking sheet.
3. Bake in the preheated oven for 20 minutes or until the sweet potato skin is lightly charred. Serve immediately.

NUTRITION: Calories: 393 Fat: 7.1g Protein: 10.2g Carbs: 76.9g

Chapter 5:
SOUP RECIPES

Basic Recipe for Vegetable Broth

Preparation time: 10 minutes.
Level: Difficult.
Cooking time: 60 minutes.
Servings: 4
INGREDIENTS:

- 8 cups water
- 1 onion, chopped
- 4 garlic cloves, crushed
- 2 celery stalks, chopped
- Pinch of salt
- 1 carrot, chopped
- Dash of pepper
- 1 potato, medium & chopped
- 1 tablespoon soy sauce
- 3 bay leaves

DIRECTIONS:

1. To make the vegetable broth, you need to place all the ingredients in a deep saucepan.
2. Heat the pan over medium-high heat. Bring the vegetable mixture to a boil.
3. Once it starts boiling, lower the heat to medium-low and allow it to simmer for at least an hour or so. Cover it with a lid.
4. When the time is up, pass it through a filter and strain the vegetables, garlic, and bay leaves.
5. Allow the stock to cool completely and store in an air-tight container.

NUTRITION: Calories: 44 Fat: 0.6g Carbs: 9.7g Protein: 0.9g

Cucumber Dill Gazpacho

Preparation time: 10 minutes.
Level: Difficult.
Cooking time: 2 hours.
Servings: 4
INGREDIENTS:

- 4 large cucumbers, peeled, seeded, and chopped
- 1/8 teaspoons salt
- 1 teaspoon chopped fresh dill + more for garnishing
- 2 tablespoons freshly squeezed lemon juice
- 1(½) cups green grape, seeds removed
- 3 tablespoons extra-virgin olive oil
- 1 garlic clove, minced

DIRECTIONS:

1. Add all the ingredients to a food processor and blend until smooth.
2. Pour the soup into serving bowls and chill for 1 to 2 hours.
3. Garnish with dill and serve chilled.

NUTRITION: Calories: 236 Fat: 1.8g Carbs: 48.3g Protein: 7g

Red Lentil Soup

Preparation time: 5 minutes.
Level: Average.
Cooking time: 25 minutes.
Servings: 4
INGREDIENTS:

- 2 tablespoons nutritional yeast
- 1 cup red lentil, washed
- ½ tablespoons garlic, minced
- 4 cups vegetable stock
- 1 teaspoon salt
- 2 cups kale, shredded
- 3 cups mixed vegetables

DIRECTIONS:

1. To start with, place all the ingredients needed to make the soup into a large pot.
2. Heat the pot over medium-high heat and bring the mixture to a boil.
3. Once it starts boiling, lower the heat to low. Allow the soup to simmer.
4. Simmer it for 1o to 15 minutes or until cooked.
5. Serve and enjoy.

NUTRITION: Calories: 212 Fat: 11.9g Carbs: 31.7g Protein: 7.3g

Spinach and Kale Soup

Preparation time: 5 minutes.
Level: Easy.
Cooking time: 5 minutes.
Servings: 4
INGREDIENTS:
- 3 ounces vegan butter
- 1 cup fresh spinach, chopped coarsely
- 1 cup fresh kale, chopped coarsely
- 1 large avocado
- 3 tablespoons chopped fresh mint leaves
- 3(½) cups coconut cream
- 1 cup vegetable broth
- Salt and black pepper to taste
- 1 lime, juiced

DIRECTIONS:
1. Melt the vegan butter in a medium pot over medium heat and sauté the kale and spinach until wilted for 3 minutes. Turn the heat off.
2. Stir in the remaining ingredients and using an immersion blender, puree the soup until smooth.
3. Dish the soup and serve warm.

NUTRITION: Calories: 380 Fat: 10g Protein: 20g Carbohydrates: 30g

Coconut and Grilled Vegetable Soup

Preparation time: 10 minutes.
Level: Difficult.
Cooking time: 45 minutes.
Servings: 4
INGREDIENTS:

- 2 small red onions cut into wedges
- 2 garlic cloves
- 10 ounces butternut squash, peeled and chopped
- 10 ounces pumpkins, peeled and chopped
- 4 tablespoons melted vegan butter
- Salt and black pepper to taste
- 1 cup of water
- 1 cup unsweetened coconut milk
- 1 lime juiced
- ¾ cup vegan mayonnaise
- Toasted pumpkin seeds for garnishing

DIRECTIONS:

1. Preheat the oven to 400°F.
2. On a baking sheet, spread the onions, garlic, butternut squash, and pumpkins and drizzle half of the butter on top. Season with salt, black pepper, and rub the seasoning well onto the vegetables. Roast in the oven for 45 minutes or until the vegetables are golden brown and softened.
3. Transfer the vegetables to a pot; add the remaining ingredients except for the pumpkin seeds and, using an immersion blender, puree the ingredients until smooth.
4. Dish the soup, garnish with the pumpkin seeds and serve warm.

NUTRITION: Calories: 290 Fat: 10g Protein: 30g Carbohydrates: 0g

Celery Dill Soup

Preparation time: 5 minutes.
Level: Average.
Cooking time: 25 minutes.
Servings: 4
INGREDIENTS:

- 2 tablespoons coconut oil
- ½ pound celery root, trimmed
- 1 garlic clove
- 1 medium white onion
- ¼ cup fresh dill, roughly chopped
- 1 teaspoon cumin powder
- ¼ teaspoons nutmeg powder
- 1 small head cauliflower, cut into florets
- 3(½) cups seasoned vegetable stock
- 5 ounces vegan butter
- Juice from 1 lemon
- ¼ cup coconut cream
- Salt and black pepper to taste

DIRECTIONS:

1. Melt the coconut oil in a large pot and sauté the celery root, garlic, and onion until softened and fragrant, 5 minutes.
2. Stir in the dill, cumin, and nutmeg, and stir-fry for 1 minute. Mix in the cauliflower and vegetable stock. Allow the soup to boil for 15 minutes and turn the heat off.
3. Add the vegan butter and lemon juice, and puree the soup using an immersion blender.
4. Stir in the coconut cream, salt, black pepper, and dish the soup. Serve warm.

NUTRITION: Calories: 320 Fat: 10g Protein: 20g Carbohydrates: 30g

Broccoli Fennel Soup

Preparation time: 15 minutes.
Level: Easy.
Cooking time: 10 minutes.
Servings: 4
INGREDIENTS:

- 1 fennel bulb, white and green parts coarsely chopped
- 10 ounces broccoli, cut into florets
- 3 cups vegetable stock
- Salt and freshly ground black pepper
- 1 garlic clove
- 1 cup dairy-free cream cheese
- 3 ounces vegan butter
- ½ cup chopped fresh oregano

DIRECTIONS:

1. In a medium pot, combine the fennel, broccoli, vegetable stock, salt, and black pepper. Bring to a boil until the vegetables soften, 10 to 15 minutes.
2. Stir in the remaining ingredients and simmer the soup for 3 to 5 minutes.
3. Adjust the taste with salt and black pepper, and dish the soup.
4. Serve warm.

NUTRITION: Calories: 240 Fat: 0g Protein: 0g Carbohydrates: 20g

Tofu Goulash Soup

Preparation time: 35 minutes.
Level: Average.
Cooking time: 20 minutes.
Servings: 4
INGREDIENTS:

- 4(¼-ounces) vegan butter
- 1 white onion, chopped
- 2 garlic cloves, minced
- 1(½) cups butternut squash
- 1 red bell pepper, seeded and chopped
- 1 tablespoon paprika powder
- ¼ teaspoon red chili flakes
- 1 tablespoon dried basil
- ½ tablespoon crushed cardamom seeds
- Salt and black pepper to taste
- 1(½) cups crushed tomatoes
- 3 cups vegetable broth
- 1(½) teaspoon red wine vinegar
- Chopped parsley to serve

DIRECTIONS:

1. Place the tofu between two paper towels and allow draining of water for 30 minutes. After, crumble the tofu and set it aside.
2. Melt the vegan butter in a large pot over medium heat and sauté the onion and garlic until the veggies are fragrant and soft, 3 minutes.
3. Stir in the tofu and cook until golden brown, 3 minutes.
4. Add the butternut squash, bell pepper, paprika, red chili flakes, basil, cardamom seeds, salt, and black pepper. Cook for 2 minutes to release some flavor and mix in the tomatoes and 2 cups of vegetable broth.
5. Close the lid, bring the soup to a boil, and then simmer for 10 minutes.
6. Stir in the remaining vegetable broth, the red wine vinegar, and adjust the taste with salt and black pepper.
7. Dish the soup, garnish with the parsley and serve warm.

NUTRITION: Calories: 320 Fat: 10g Protein: 10g Carbohydrates: 20g

Pesto Pea Soup

Preparation time: 10 minutes.
Level: Average.
Cooking time: 20 minutes.
Servings: 4
INGREDIENTS:

- 2 cups water
- 8 ounces tortellini
- ¼ cup pesto
- 1 onion, small & finely chopped
- 1 pound peas, frozen
- 1 carrot, medium & finely chopped
- 1 ¾ cup vegetable broth, less sodium
- 1 celery rib, medium & finely chopped

DIRECTIONS:

1. To start with, boil the water into a large pot over medium-high heat.
2. Next, stir in the tortellini to the pot and cook it following the packet's instructions.
3. In the meantime, cook the onion, celery, and carrot in a deep saucepan along with the water and broth.
4. Cook the celery-onion mixture for 6 minutes or until softened.
5. Now, spoon in the peas and allow them to simmer while keeping them uncovered.
6. Cook the peas for few minutes or until they are bright green and soft.
7. Then, spoon in the pesto to the pea's mixture. Combine well.
8. Pour the mixture into a high-speed blender and blend for 2 to 3 minutes or until you get a rich, smooth soup.
9. Return the soup to the pan. Spoon in the cooked tortellini.
10. Finally, pour into a serving bowl and top with more cooked peas if desired.
11. **Tip:** If desired, you can season it with Maldon salt at the end.

NUTRITION: Calories: 100 Fat: 0g Protein: 0g Carbohydrates: 0g

Tofu and Mushroom Soup

Preparation time: 15 minutes.
Level: Easy.
Cooking time: 10 minutes.
Servings: 4
INGREDIENTS:

- 2 tablespoons olive oil
- 1 garlic clove, minced
- 1 large yellow onion, finely chopped
- 1 teaspoon freshly grated ginger
- 1 cup vegetable stock
- 2 small potatoes, peeled and chopped
- ¼ teaspoon salt
- ¼ teaspoon black pepper
- 2 (14-ounces) silken tofu, drained and rinsed
- 2/3 cup baby Bella mushrooms, sliced
- 1 tablespoon chopped fresh oregano
- 2 tablespoons chopped fresh parsley to garnish

DIRECTIONS:

1. Heat the olive oil in a medium pot over medium heat and sauté the garlic, onion, and ginger until soft and fragrant.
2. Pour in the vegetable stock, potatoes, salt, and black pepper. Cook until the potatoes soften, 12 minutes.
3. Stir in the tofu and using an immersion blender, puree the ingredients until smooth.
4. Mix in the mushrooms and simmer with the pot covered until the mushrooms warm up while occasionally stirring to ensure that the tofu doesn't curdle for 7 minutes.
5. Stir oregano, and dish the soup.
6. Garnish with the parsley and serve warm.

NUTRITION: Calories: 310 Fat: 10g Protein: 40.0g Carbohydrates: 0g

Moroccan Vermicelli Vegetable Soup

Preparation time: 5 minutes.
Level: Average.
Cooking time: 35 minutes.
Servings: 4
INGREDIENTS:

- 1 tablespoon olive oil
- 1 small onion, chopped
- 1 large carrot, chopped
- 1 celery rib, chopped
- 3 small zucchinis, cut into 1/4-inch dice
- 1(28-ounce) can diced tomatoes, drained
- 2 tablespoons tomato paste
- 1(1/2) cups cooked or 1 (15.5-ounce) can chickpeas, drained and rinsed
- 2 teaspoons smoked paprika
- 1 teaspoon ground cumin
- 1 teaspoon za'atar spice (optional)
- 1/4 teaspoon ground cayenne
- 6 cups vegetable broth, homemade (see light vegetable broth) or store-bought, or water
- Salt to taste
- 4 ounces vermicelli
- 2 tablespoons minced fresh cilantro, for garnish

DIRECTIONS:

1. In a large soup pot, heat the oil over medium heat. Add the onion, carrot, and celery. Cover and cook until softened about 5 minutes. Stir in the zucchini, tomatoes, tomato paste, chickpeas, paprika, cumin, za'atar, and cayenne.
2. Add the broth and salt to taste. Bring to a boil, then reduce heat to low and simmer, uncovered, until the vegetables are tender about 30 minutes.
3. Shortly before serving, stir in the vermicelli and cook until the noodles are tender about 5 minutes. Ladle the soup into bowls, garnish with cilantro, and serve.

NUTRITION: Calories: 236 Fat: 1.8g Carbs: 48.3g Protein: 7g

Moroccan Vegetable Stew

Preparation time: 5 minutes.
Level: Average.
Cooking time: 35 minutes.
Servings: 4
INGREDIENTS:

- 1 tablespoon olive oil
- 2 medium yellow onions, chopped
- 2 medium carrots, cut into 1/2-inch dice
- 1/2 teaspoon ground cumin
- 1/2 teaspoon ground cinnamon or allspice
- 1/2 teaspoon ground ginger
- 1/2 teaspoon sweet or smoked paprika
- 1/2 teaspoon saffron or turmeric
- 1 (14.5-ounce) can diced tomatoes, undrained
- 8 ounces green beans, trimmed and cut into 1-inch pieces
- 2 cups peeled, seeded, and diced winter squash
- 1 large russet or other baking potatoes, peeled and cut into 1/2-inch dice
- 1(1/2) cups vegetable broth
- 1(1/2) cups cooked or 1(15.5-ounce) can chickpeas, drained and rinsed
- ¾ cup frozen peas
- 1/2 cup pitted dried plums (prunes)
- 1 teaspoon lemon zest
- Salt and freshly ground black pepper
- 1/2 cup pitted green olives
- 1 tablespoon minced fresh cilantro or parsley, for garnish
- 1/2 cup toasted slivered almonds, for garnish

DIRECTIONS:

1. In a large saucepan, heat the oil over medium heat. Add the onions and carrots, cover, and cook for 5 minutes. Stir in the cumin, cinnamon, ginger, paprika, and saffron. Cook, uncovered, stirring, for 30 seconds.
2. Add the tomatoes, green beans, squash, potato, and broth and bring to a boil. Reduce heat to low, cover, and simmer until the vegetables are tender about 20 minutes.
3. Add the chickpeas, peas, dried plums, and lemon zest. Season with salt and pepper to taste. Stir in the olives and simmer, uncovered, until the flavors are blended for about 10 minutes. Sprinkle with cilantro and almonds and serve immediately.

NUTRITION: Calories: 71 Fat: 2.8g Carbs: 9.8g Protein: 3.7g

Avocado Cucumber Soup

Preparation time: 20 minutes.
Level: Easy.
Cooking time: 0 minutes.
Servings: 4
INGREDIENTS:

- 1 large cucumber, peeled and sliced
- ¾ cup water
- ¼ cup lemon juice
- 2 garlic cloves
- 6 green onion
- 2 avocados, pitted
- ½ teaspoons black pepper
- ½ teaspoons pink salt

DIRECTIONS:

1. Add all the ingredients into the blender and blend until smooth and creamy.
2. Place in refrigerator for 30 minutes.
3. Stir well and serve chilled.

NUTRITION: Calories: 127 Fat: 6.6g Carbs: 13g Protein: 0.7g

Garden Vegetable Stew

Preparation time: 5 minutes.
Level: Difficult.
Cooking time: 60 minutes.
Servings: 4
INGREDIENTS:

- 2 tablespoons olive oil
- 1 medium red onion, chopped
- 1 medium carrot, cut into 1/4-inch slices
- 1/2 cup dry white wine
- 3 medium new potatoes, unpeeled and cut into 1-inch pieces
- 1 medium red bell pepper, cut into 1/2-inch dice
- 1(1/2) cups vegetable broth
- 1 tablespoon minced fresh savory or 1 teaspoon dried
- 2 Zucchini
- 2 Yellow squash
- 1 cup Tomatoes
- 2 Corn
- 1 cup Peas
- 1 cup Basil
- ½ cup Parsley

DIRECTIONS:

1. In a large saucepan, heat the oil over medium heat. Add the onion and carrot, cover, and cook until softened, 7 minutes. Add the wine and cook, uncovered, for 5 minutes. Stir in the potatoes, bell pepper, and broth and bring to a boil. Reduce the heat to medium and simmer for 15 minutes.
2. Add the zucchini, yellow squash, and tomatoes. Season with salt and black pepper to taste, cover, and simmer until the vegetables are tender, 20 to 30 minutes. Stir in the corn, peas, basil, parsley, and savory. Taste, adjusting seasonings if necessary. Simmer to blend flavors for about 10 minutes more. Serve immediately.

NUTRITION: Calories: 219 Fat: 4.5g Carbs: 38.2g Protein: 6.4g

Lemon and Egg Soup

Preparation time: 15 minutes.
Level: Easy.
Cooking time: 0 minutes.
Servings: 4

INGREDIENTS:

- 4 cups fat-free and low-sodium chicken broth
- 2 large whole eggs
- ½ cup fresh lemon juice
- 4 tablespoons chopped fresh parsley
- 1 lemon, thinly sliced for garnish
- Salt and freshly ground pepper to taste

DIRECTIONS

1. Place a medium saucepan on medium-high heat. Add chicken broth to it and bring it to a boil, stirring it a couple of times.
2. Bring down the heat to low and allow the broth to simmer for about 5 minutes. Take the saucepan off the heat.
3. Take a bowl and add the eggs to it. Beat them well, add the lemon juice, and beat the eggs again
4. Use a ladle to transfer a single serving of the chicken broth into the egg bowl. Mix them well and then transfer the entire contents of the bowl into the saucepan.
5. Heat the soup while ensuring that the heat is still at a low. Keep an eye out on the eggs because they tend to curdle and you need to prevent that from happening by gently stirring the soup.
6. Add salt and pepper to taste, if preferred.
7. Serve hot and garnish with lemon slices and parsley.

NUTRITION: Calories: 161 Protein: 10g Fat: 2g Carbohydrate: 65g

Roasted Vegetable Soup

Preparation time: 15 minutes.
Level: Average.
Cooking time: 20 minutes.
Servings: 4
INGREDIENTS:

- 1 tablespoon olive oil
- 5 garlic cloves, peeled
- 0.3pounds Potatoes diced (1 cm thick)
- 2 yellow bell peppers, diced
- ½ teaspoons fresh rosemary, finely chopped
- 1 carrot, halved lengthwise and cut into 1 cm piece
- 1 red onion, in chunks
- 0.4 quarts carrot juice
- 0.3pounds Italian tomatoes, diced
- 1 teaspoon fresh tarragon
- Salt and pepper, to taste

DIRECTIONS:

1. Preheat the oven to 400° F.
2. In a baking tray place potatoes, peppers, garlic, carrot, onion, and tomatoes. Drizzle with olive oil and roast for 10–15 minutes.
3. In a saucepan add carrot juice, tarragon; let boil a little.
4. Add all roasted vegetables and stir well. Let it simmer for a few minutes.
5. Season with salt, pepper, and rosemary. Mix well.
6. Serve and enjoy.

NUTRITION: Calories: 318 Fat: 97g Carbs: 60g Protein: 1.7g

Mediterranean Tomato Soup

Preparation time: 5 minutes.
Level: Difficult.
Cooking time: 30 minutes.
Servings: 4
INGREDIENT:

- 2 red bell peppers, unseeded, chopped
- 2 medium onions, chopped
- 2-3 garlic cloves, minced
- 7–8 tomatoes, chopped
- 0.4 quarts chicken broth
- Salt and pepper, to taste
- 3 tablespoons olive oil
- 1 tablespoon vinegar

DIRECTIONS:

1. Heat oil in a saucepan and cook onion, garlic, and bell peppers for 5–6 minutes or until bell peppers are roasted well.
2. Add tomatoes, salt, pepper, and vinegar; stir-fry for 4–5 minutes.
3. Add chicken broth and cover with lid. Let it cook for about 20 minutes on low heat.
4. When tomatoes are cooked well, puree the soup with the help of an electric beater.
5. Simmer for 1–2 minutes.
6. Add to a serving dish and top with desired herbs.
7. Serve and enjoy.

NUTRITION: Calories: 318 Fat: 97g Carbs: 60g Protein: 1.7g

Tomato and Cabbage Puree Soup

Preparation time: 5 minutes.
Level: Difficult.
Cooking time: 30 minutes.
Servings: 4
INGREDIENTS:

- 0.6 pounds tomatoes, chopped
- 3-4 garlic cloves, minced
- 0.2 pounds Cabbage, chopped
- 4 tablespoons olive oil
- 1 red onion, chopped
- Salt and pepper to taste
- Spice mix of choice
- 4 quarts of vegetable broth

DIRECTIONS:

1. Heat oil in a saucepan and cook onion, garlic, and cabbage for about 4–5 minutes. Make sure that cabbage is nicely softened.
2. Add tomatoes and stir-fry until liquid is reduced and tomatoes are dissolved.
3. Add salt, pepper, spice mix, and vegetable broth.
4. Cover the saucepan with a lid and let the mixture cook on low flame for about 30 minutes.
5. Puree the soup with the help of an electric beater.
6. Serve and enjoy.

NUTRITION: Calories: 218 Fat: 15g Carbs: 220g Protein: 2g

Athenian Avgolemono Sour Soup

Preparation time: 20 minutes.
Level: Difficult.
Cooking time: 50 minutes.
Servings: 4
INGREDIENTS:

- 8-cups water
- 1 piece whole chicken, cut into pieces
- Salt and pepper
- 1-cup whole-grain rice
- 4 pieces eggs, separated
- 2 pieces lemons, juice
- ¼-cup fresh dill, minced
- Dill sprigs and lemon slices for garnish

DIRECTIONS:

1. Pour the water into a large pot. Add the chicken pieces and cover the pot. Simmer for an hour
2. Remove the cooked chicken pieces from the pot and take 2-cups of the chicken broth. Set aside and let it cool
3. Bring to a boil the remaining. Add salt and pepper to taste. Add the rice and cover the pot. Simmer for 20 minutes
4. Meanwhile, de-bone the cooked chicken and tear the flesh into small pieces. Set aside.
5. Work on the separated egg whites and yolks: whisk the egg whites until stiff; whisk the yolks with the lemon juice.
6. Pour the egg yolk mixture into the egg white mixture. Whisk well until fully combined.
7. Add gradually the reserved 2-cups of chicken broth to the mixture, whisking constantly to prevent the eggs from curdling.
8. After fully incorporating the egg mixture and chicken broth, pour this mixture into the simmering broth and rice. Add the dill, and stir well. Simmer further without bringing it to a boil.
9. Add the chicken pieces to the soup. Mix until fully combined.
10. To serve, ladle the soup in bowls and sprinkle with freshly ground pepper. Garnish with lemon slices and dill sprigs.

NUTRITION: Calories: 122.4 Fats: 1.2g Dietary fiber: 0.2g Carbohydrates: 7.5g Protein: 13.7g

Mediterranean Diet Cookbook For Beginners

Italian Bean Soup

Preparation time: 15 minutes.
Level: Easy.
Cooking time: 15 minutes.
Servings: 4
INGREDIENTS:

- 1 tablespoon virgin olive oil
- 1 onion (diced)
- 2 garlic cloves (minced)
- 2 cups tomato sauce (homemade or 1 can of low-sodium organic canned tomato sauce)
- 3 cups cooked cannellini beans (or about 24 ounces of canned beans that have been drained and rinsed)
- 1 tablespoon basil (dried)
- ½ teaspoon oregano
- ¼ teaspoon black pepper

DIRECTIONS:

1. Take a large soup or stockpot and place it on your stove. Turn the heat all the way up to medium-high and pour in the virgin olive oil.
2. Allow the oil to heat slightly before adding your diced onions to the pot. Sautee for 3 minutes and then add the garlic. Let the flavors come together for 2 minutes.
3. Add the cannellini beans, basil, oregano, and black pepper to the pot. Stir everything together, then pour over the tomato sauce.
4. Allow the sauce to come to a steady simmer. Reduce the heat to medium-low. Cover your pot so the flavors can simmer together for 5 minutes.
5. Uncover the pot and allow the aroma to fill your kitchen. Then, take a ladle and fill your soup bowls! Grab a soup spoon and enjoy

NUTRITION: Calories: 164 Carbs: 25.6g Protein: 8.1g Fat: 3.8g

71

Chapter 6:
PIZZA RECIPES

Pizza Bianca

Preparation time: 10 minutes.
Level: Easy.
Cooking time: 10 minutes.
Servings: 4
INGREDIENTS:

- 2 tablespoons olive oil
- 4 eggs
- 2 tablespoons water
- 1 jalapeno pepper, diced
- 1/4 cup mozzarella cheese, shredded
- 2 chives, chopped
- 2 cups Alfredo sauce
- 1/2 teaspoons oregano
- 1/2 cup mushrooms, sliced

DIRECTIONS:
1. Preheat the oven to 360°F.
2. In a bowl, whisk eggs, water, and oregano. Heat the olive oil in a large skillet.
3. The egg mixture must be poured in then let it cook until set, flipping once.
4. Remove and spread the Alfredo sauce and jalapeno pepper all over.
5. Top with mozzarella cheese, mushrooms and chives. Let it bake for 10 minutes

NUTRITION: Calories: 314 Fat: 15.6g Fiber: 10.3g Carbohydrates: 5.9g Protein: 10.4g

Eggplant Pizza with Tofu

Preparation time: 15 minutes.
Level: Difficult.
Cooking time: 45 minutes.
Servings: 4
INGREDIENTS:

- 2 eggplants, sliced
- 1/3 cup butter, melted
- 2 garlic cloves, minced
- 1 Red onion
- 12 ounces tofu, chopped
- 2 Ounces tomato sauce
- Salt and black pepper to taste
- 1/2 teaspoon cinnamon powder
- 1 cup parmesan cheese, shredded
- 1/4 cup dried oregano

DIRECTIONS:

1. Let the oven heat to 400°F. Lay the eggplant slices on a baking sheet and brush with some butter. Bake in the oven until lightly browned about 20 minutes.
2. Heat the remaining butter in a skillet; sauté garlic and onion until fragrant and soft about 3 minutes.
3. Stir in the tofu and cook for 3 minutes. Add the tomato sauce, salt, and black pepper. Simmer for 10 minutes.
4. Sprinkle with Parmesan cheese and oregano. Bake for 10 minutes.

NUTRITION: Calories: 321 Fat: 11.3g Fiber: 8.4g Carbohydrates: 4.3g Protein: 10.1g

Thin Crust Low Carb Pizza

Preparation time: 15 minutes.
Level: Average.
Cooking time: 25 minutes.
Servings: 4
INGREDIENTS:

- 2 tablespoons tomato sauce
- 1/8 teaspoon black pepper
- 1/8 teaspoon chili flakes
- 1 piece low-carb pita bread
- 2 ounces low-moisture mozzarella cheese
- 1/8 teaspoon garlic powder

Toppings:

- Bacon, roasted red peppers, spinach, olives, pesto, artichokes, salami, pepperoni, roast beef, prosciutto, avocado, ham, chili paste, Sriracha

DIRECTIONS:

1. Warm the oven to 450°F, then oiled a baking dish. Mix tomato sauce, black pepper, chili flakes, and garlic powder in a bowl and keep aside.
2. Place the low-carb pita bread in the oven and bake for about 2 minutes. Remove from the oven and spread the tomato sauce on it.
3. Add mozzarella cheese and top with your favorite toppings. Bake again for 3 minutes and dish out.

NUTRITION: Calories: 254 Carbs: 12.9g Fats: 16g Proteins: 19.3g

BBQ Chicken Pizza

Preparation time: 15 minutes.
Level: Average.
Cooking time: 30 minutes.
Servings: 4
INGREDIENTS:
Dairy-Free Pizza Crust:

- 6 tablespoons Parmesan cheese
- 6 large eggs
- 3 tablespoons psyllium husk powder
- Salt and black pepper, to taste
- 1(½) teaspoon Italian seasoning

Toppings:

- 6 ounces rotisserie chicken, shredded
- 4 ounces cheddar cheese
- 1 tablespoon mayonnaise
- 4 tablespoons tomato sauce
- 4 tablespoons BBQ sauce

DIRECTIONS:

1. Warm the oven to 400°F and grease a baking dish. Place all the pizza crust ingredients in an immersion blender and blend until smooth.
2. Spread dough mixture onto the baking dish and transfer it to the oven. Bake for about 10 minutes and top with favorite toppings. Bake for about 3 minutes and dish out.

NUTRITION: Calories: 356 Carbs: 2.9g Fats: 24.5g Proteins: 24.5g

Chapter 7:
VEGETABLE RECIPES

Vegetarian Chili with Avocado Cream

Preparation time: 15 minutes.
Level: Average.
Cooking time: 25 minutes.
Servings: 4
INGREDIENTS:
- 2 tablespoons olive oil
- 1/2 onion, finely chopped
- 1 Tablespoon minced garlic
- 1 Jalapeno peppers, chopped
- 1 1Red bell pepper, diced
- 1 Teaspoon ground cumin
- 1 1Tablespoons chili powder
- 1 Cups pecans, chopped
- 1 Cups canned diced tomatoes and their juice

Topping:
- 1 cup sour cream
- 1 avocado, diced
- 2 tablespoons fresh cilantro, chopped

DIRECTIONS:
1. Heat olive oil.
2. Toss in the onion, garlic, jalapeno peppers, and red bell pepper, then sauté for about 4 minutes until tender.
3. Put in the chili powder and cumin and stir for 30 seconds.
4. Fold in the pecans, tomatoes, and their juice, then bring to a boil.
5. Simmer uncovered for about 20 minutes to infuse the flavors, stirring occasionally.
6. Remove from the heat to eight bowls.
7. Evenly top each bowl of chili with sour cream, diced avocado, and fresh cilantro.

NUTRITION: Calories: 318 Fat: 14.4g Fiber: 17.5g Carbohydrates: 9.5g Protein: 14g

Eggs with Zucchini Noodles

Preparation time: 10 minutes.
Level: Average.
Cooking time: 11 minutes.
Servings: 4
INGREDIENTS:

- 2 tablespoons extra-virgin olive oil
- 3 zucchinis, cut with a spiralizer
- 4 eggs
- Salt and black pepper to taste
- A pinch of red pepper flakes
- Cooking spray
- 1 tablespoon basil, chopped

DIRECTIONS:

1. In a bowl, combine the zucchini noodles with salt, pepper, and olive oil and toss well.
2. Grease a baking sheet with cooking spray and divide the zucchini noodles into 4 nests.
3. Crack an egg on top of each nest, sprinkle salt, pepper, and pepper flakes on top and bake at 350°F for 11 minutes.
4. Divide the mix between plates, sprinkle the basil on top, and serve.

NUTRITION: Calories: 296 Fat: 23.6 Fiber: 3.3 Carbs: 10.6 Protein: 14.7

Roasted Root Veggies

Preparation time: 20 minutes.
Level: Difficult.
Cooking time: 1 hour and 30 minutes.
Servings: 4
INGREDIENTS:

- 2 tablespoons olive oil
- 1 head garlic, cloves separated and peeled
- 1 large turnip, peeled and cut into ½-inch pieces
- 1 medium-sized red onion, cut into ½-inch pieces
- 1(½) pound beets, trimmed but not peeled, scrubbed, and cut into ½-inch pieces
- 1(½) pound Yukon gold potatoes, unpeeled, cut into ½-inch pieces
- 2(½) pounds butternut squash, peeled, seeded, cut into ½-inch pieces

DIRECTIONS:

1. Grease 2 rimmed and large baking sheets. Preheat the oven to 425°F.
2. In a large bowl, mix all the ingredients thoroughly.
3. Into the two baking sheets, evenly divide the root vegetables, spread in one layer.
4. Season generously with pepper and salt.
5. Pop into the oven and roast for 1 hour and 15 minutes or until golden brown and tender.
6. Remove from the oven and let it cool for at least 15 minutes before serving.

NUTRITION: Calories: 298 Carbs: 61.1g Protein: 7.4g Fat: 5.0g

Rustic Vegetable and Brown Rice Bowl

Preparation time: 15 minutes.
Level: Easy.
Cooking time: 10 minutes.
Servings: 4
INGREDIENTS:
- Nonstick cooking spray
- 2 cups broccoli florets
- 2 cups cauliflower florets
- 1(15-ounces) can chickpeas, drained and rinsed
- 1 cup carrots sliced 1 inch thick
- 2 to 3 tablespoons extra-virgin olive oil, divided
- Salt and freshly ground black pepper
- 2 to 3 tablespoons sesame seeds, for garnish
- 2 cups cooked brown rice

For the dressing
- 3 to 4 tablespoons tahini
- 2 tablespoons honey
- 1 lemon, juiced
- 1 garlic clove, minced
- Salt to taste
- Freshly ground black pepper to taste

DIRECTIONS:
1. Preheat the oven to 400°F. Spray two baking sheets with cooking spray.
2. Cover the first baking sheet with broccoli and cauliflower and the second with chickpeas and carrots. Toss each sheet with half of the oil and season with salt and pepper before placing it in the oven.
3. Cook the carrots and chickpeas for 10 minutes, leaving the carrots still just crisp, and the broccoli and cauliflower for 20 minutes, until tender. Stir each halfway through cooking.
4. To make the dressing, in a small bowl, mix the tahini, honey, lemon juice, and garlic. Season with salt and pepper and set aside.
5. Divide the rice into individual bowls, then layer with vegetables and drizzle dressing over the dish.

NUTRITION: Calories: 192 Carbs: 12.7g Protein: 3.8g Fat: 15.5g

Roasted Brussels Sprouts and Pecans

Preparation time: 10 minutes.
Level: Easy.
Cooking time: 15 minutes.
Servings: 4
INGREDIENTS:

- 1(½) pound fresh Brussels sprouts
- 4 tablespoons olive oil
- 4 cloves of garlic, minced
- 3 tablespoons water
- Salt and pepper to taste
- ½ cup chopped pecans

DIRECTIONS:

1. Place all the ingredients in the Instant Pot.
2. Combine all the ingredients until well combined.
3. Close the lid and make sure that the steam release vent is set to "Venting."
4. Press the "Slow Cook" button and adjust the cooking time to 3 hours.
5. Sprinkle with a dash of lemon juice if desired.

NUTRITION: Calories: 161 Carbs: 10.2g Protein: 4.1g Fat: 13.1g

Roasted Vegetables and Zucchini Pasta

Preparation time: 10 minutes.
Level: Easy.
Cooking time: 7 minutes.
Servings: 4
INGREDIENTS:

- ¼ cup raw pine nuts
- 4 cups leftover vegetables
- 2 garlic cloves, minced
- 1 tablespoon extra-virgin olive oil
- 4 medium zucchinis, cut into long strips resembling noodles

DIRECTIONS:

1. Heat oil in a large skillet over medium heat and sauté the garlic for 2 minutes.
2. Add the leftover vegetables and place the zucchini noodles on top. Let it cook for five minutes. Garnish with pine nuts.

NUTRITION: Calories: 288 Carbs: 23.6g Protein: 8.2g Fat: 19.2g

Sautéed Collard Greens

Preparation time: 10 minutes.
Level: Easy.
Cooking time: 0 minutes.
Servings: 4
INGREDIENTS:

- 1 pound fresh collard greens, cut into 2-inch pieces
- 1 pinch red pepper flakes
- 3 cups chicken broth
- 1 teaspoon pepper
- 1 teaspoon salt
- 2 cloves garlic, minced
- 1 large onion, chopped
- 3 slices bacon
- 1 tablespoon olive oil

DIRECTIONS:

1. Using a large skillet, heat oil on medium-high heat. Sauté bacon until crisp. Remove it from the pan and crumble it once cooled. Set it aside.
2. Using the same pan, sauté onion and cook until tender. Add garlic until fragrant. Add the collard greens and cook until they start to wilt.
3. Pour in the chicken broth and season with pepper, salt, and red pepper flakes. Reduce the heat to low and simmer for 45 minutes.

NUTRITION: Calories: 20 Carbs: 3.0g Protein: 1.0g Fat: 1.0g

Balsamic Bulgur Salad

Preparation time: 30 minutes.
Level: Easy.
Cooking time: 0 minutes.
Servings: 4
INGREDIENTS:

- 1 cup bulgur
- 2 cups hot water
- 1 cucumber, sliced
- A pinch of sea salt and black pepper
- 2 tablespoons lemon juice
- 2 tablespoons balsamic vinegar
- ¼ cup olive oil

DIRECTIONS:

1. In a bowl, mix bulgur with the water, cover, leave aside for 30 minutes, fluff with a fork, and transfer to a salad bowl. Add the rest of the ingredients, toss and serve.

NUTRITION: Calories: 171 Fat: 5.1g Fiber: 6.1g Carbs: 11.3g Protein: 4.4g

Savoy Cabbage with Coconut Cream Sauce

Preparation time: 5 minutes.
Level: Average.
Cooking time: 20 minutes.
Servings: 4

INGREDIENTS:

- 3 tablespoons olive oil
- 1 onion, chopped
- 4 cloves of garlic, minced
- 1 head savoy cabbage, chopped finely
- 2 cups bone broth
- 1 cup coconut milk, freshly squeezed
- 1 bay leaf
- Salt and pepper to taste
- 2 tablespoons chopped parsley

DIRECTIONS:

1. Heat oil in a pot for 2 minutes.
2. Stir in the onions, bay leaf, and garlic until fragrant, around 3 minutes.
3. Add the rest of the ingredients, except for the parsley, and mix well.
4. Cover pot, bring to a boil, and let it simmer for 5 minutes or until cabbage is tender to taste.
5. Stir in parsley and serve.

NUTRITION: Calories: 195 Carbs: 12.3g Protein: 2.7g Fat: 19.7g

Slow-Cooked Buttery Mushrooms

Preparation time: 10 minutes.
Level: Easy.
Cooking time: 10 minutes.
Servings: 4
INGREDIENTS:

- 2 tablespoons butter
- 2 tablespoons olive oil
- 3 cloves of garlic, minced
- 16 ounces fresh brown mushrooms, sliced
- 7 ounces fresh shiitake mushrooms, sliced
- A dash of thyme
- Salt and pepper to taste

DIRECTIONS:

1. Heat the butter and oil in a pot.
2. Sauté the garlic until fragrant, around 1 minute.
3. Stir in the rest of the ingredients and cook until soft, around 9 minutes.

NUTRITION: Calories: 192 Carbs: 12.7g Protein: 3.8g Fat: 15.5g

Radish and Corn Salad

Preparation time: 10 minutes.
Level: Easy.
Cooking time: 0 minutes.
Servings: 4
INGREDIENTS:

- 1 tablespoon lemon juice
- 1 jalapeno, chopped
- 2 tablespoons olive oil
- ¼ teaspoon oregano, dried
- A pinch of sea salt and black pepper
- 2 cups fresh corn
- 6 radishes, sliced

DIRECTIONS:

1. In a salad bowl, combine the corn with the radishes and the rest of the ingredients, toss, and serve cold.

NUTRITION: Calories: 134 Fat: 4.5g Fiber: 1.8g Carbs: 4.1g Protein: 1.9g

Arugula and Corn Salad

Preparation time: 10 minutes.
Level: Easy.
Cooking time: 0 minutes.
Servings: 4
INGREDIENTS:

- 1 red bell pepper, thinly sliced
- 2 cups corn
- Juice of 1 lime
- Zest of 1 lime, grated
- 8 cups baby arugula
- A pinch of sea salt and black pepper

DIRECTIONS:

1. In a salad bowl, mix the corn with the arugula and the rest of the ingredients, toss and serve cold.

NUTRITION: Calories: 172 Fat: 8.5g Fiber: 1.8g Carbs: 5.1g Protein: 1.4g

Steamed Squash Chowder

Preparation time: 20 minutes.
Level: Difficult.
Cooking time: 40 minutes.
Servings: 4

INGREDIENTS:

- 3 cups chicken broth
- 2 tablespoons ghee
- 1 teaspoon chili powder
- ½ teaspoon cumin
- 1(½) teaspoon salt
- 2 teaspoons cinnamon
- 3 tablespoons olive oil
- 2 carrots, chopped
- 1 small yellow onion, chopped
- 1 green apple, sliced and cored
- 1 large butternut squash, peeled, seeded, and chopped to ½-inch cubes

DIRECTIONS:

1. In a large pot on medium-high fire, melt ghee.
2. Once the ghee is hot, sauté onions for 5 minutes or until soft and translucent.
3. Add olive oil, chili powder, cumin, salt, and cinnamon. Sauté for half a minute.
4. Add chopped squash and apples.
5. Sauté for 10 minutes while stirring once in a while.
6. Add broth, cover, and cook on medium fire for twenty minutes or until apples and squash are tender.
7. With an immersion blender, puree chowder. Adjust consistency by adding more water.
8. Add more salt or pepper depending as desired.
9. Serve and enjoy.

NUTRITION: Calories: 228 Carbs: 17.9g Protein: 2.2g Fat: 18.0g

Steamed Zucchini-Paprika

Preparation time: 15 minutes.
Level: Average.
Cooking time: 30 minutes.
Servings: 4
INGREDIENTS:

- 4 tablespoons olive oil
- 3 cloves of garlic, minced
- 1 onion, chopped
- 3 medium-sized zucchinis, sliced thinly
- A dash of paprika
- Salt and pepper to taste

DIRECTIONS:

1. Place all the ingredients in the Instant Pot. Give a good stir to combine all the ingredients.
2. Close the lid and make sure that the steam release valve is set to "Venting."
3. Press the "Slow Cook" button and adjust the cooking time to 4 hours.
4. Halfway through the cooking time, open the lid and give a good stir to brown the other side.

NUTRITION: Calories: 93 Carbs: 3.1g Protein: 0.6g Fat: 10.2g

Orange and Cucumber Salad

Preparation time: 10 minutes.
Level: Easy.
Cooking time: 0 minutes.
Servings: 4
INGREDIENTS:

- 2 cucumbers, sliced
- 1 orange, peeled, and cut into segments
- 1 cup cherry tomatoes, halved
- 1 small red onion, chopped
- 3 tablespoons olive oil
- 4(½) teaspoons balsamic vinegar
- Salt and black pepper to taste
- 1 tablespoon lemon juice

DIRECTIONS:

1. In a bowl, mix the cucumbers with the orange and the rest of the ingredients, toss and serve cold.

NUTRITION: Calories: 102 Fat: 7.5g Fiber: 3g Carbs: 6.1g Protein: 3.4g

Parsley and Corn Salad

Preparation time: 10 minutes.
Level: Easy.
Cooking time: 0 minutes.
Servings: 4
INGREDIENTS:
- 1(½) teaspoon balsamic vinegar
- 2 tablespoons lime juice
- 2 tablespoons olive oil
- A pinch of sea salt and black pepper
- Black pepper to taste
- 4 cups corn
- ½ cup parsley, chopped
- 2 spring onions, chopped

DIRECTIONS:
1. In a salad bowl, combine the corn with the onions and the rest of the ingredients, toss, and serve cold.

NUTRITION: Calories: 121 Fat: 9.5g Fiber: 1.8g Carbs: 4.1g Protein: 1.9g

Stir-Fried Brussels Sprouts and Carrots

Preparation time: 10 minutes.
Level: Easy.
Cooking time: 15 minutes.
Servings: 4
INGREDIENTS:

- 1 tablespoon cider vinegar
- 1/3 cup water
- 1 pound Brussels sprouts halved lengthwise
- 1 pound carrots cut diagonally into ½-inch thick lengths
- 3 tablespoons unsalted butter, divided
- 2 tablespoons chopped shallot
- ½ teaspoon pepper
- ¾ teaspoon salt

DIRECTIONS:

1. On medium-high fire, place a nonstick medium fry pan and heat 2 tablespoons of butter.
2. Add shallots and cook until softened, around 1–2 minutes while occasionally stirring.
3. Add pepper, salt, Brussels sprouts, and carrots. Stir-fry until vegetables start to brown on the edges, around 3 to 4 minutes.
4. Add water, cook, and cover.
5. After 5 to 8 minutes, or when veggies are already soft, add the remaining butter.
6. If needed, season with more pepper and salt to taste.
7. Turn off the fire, transfer to a platter, serve and enjoy.

NUTRITION: Calories: 98 Carbs: 13.9g Protein: 3.5g Fat: 4.2g

Stir-Fried Eggplant

Preparation time: 10 minutes.
Level: Average.
Cooking time: 30 minutes.
Servings: 4
INGREDIENTS:

- 1 teaspoon cornstarch + 2 tablespoons water, mixed
- 1 teaspoon brown sugar
- 2 tablespoons oyster sauce
- 1 tablespoon fish sauce
- 2 tablespoons soy sauce
- ½ cup fresh basil
- 2 tablespoons oil
- ¼ cup water
- 2 cups Chinese eggplant, spiral
- 1 red chili
- 6 cloves garlic, minced
- ½ purple onion, sliced thinly
- 1(3-ounces) package medium-firm tofu, cut into slivers

DIRECTIONS:

1. Prepare sauce by mixing cornstarch and water in a small bowl. In another bowl mix brown sugar, oyster sauce, and fish sauce and set aside.
2. On medium-high fire, place a large nonstick saucepan and heat 2 tablespoons of oil. Sauté chili, garlic, and onion for 4 minutes. Add tofu, stir-fry for 4 minutes.
3. Add eggplant noodles and stir-fry for 10 minutes. If the pan dries up, add water in small amounts to moisten into the pan and cook noodles.
4. Pour in the sauce and mix well. Once simmering, slowly add cornstarch mixer while continuing to mix vigorously. Once the sauce thickens, add fresh basil and cook for a minute.
5. Remove from fire, transfer to a serving plate and enjoy.

NUTRITION: Calories: 369 Carbs: 28.4g Protein: 11.4g Fat: 25.3g

Tomato and Avocado Salad

Preparation time: 10 minutes.
Level: Easy.
Cooking time: 0 minutes.
Servings: 4
INGREDIENTS:

- 1 pound cherry tomatoes, cubed
- 2 avocados, pitted, peeled, and cubed
- 1 sweet onion, chopped
- A pinch of sea salt and black pepper
- 2 tablespoons lemon juice
- 1(½) tablespoon olive oil
- A handful of basil, chopped

DIRECTIONS:

1. In a salad bowl, mix the tomatoes with the avocados and the rest of the ingredients, toss and serve right away.

NUTRITION: Calories: 148 Fat: 7.8g Fiber: 2.9g Carbs: 5.4g Protein: 5.5g

Avocado and Tomato Salad

Preparation Time: 10 minutes.
Level: Easy.
Cooking time: 0 minutes.
Servings: 4
INGREDIENTS:

- 2 avocados, pitted, peeled, and cubed
- 1-pint mixed cherry tomatoes halved
- 2 tablespoons avocado oil
- 1 tablespoon lime juice
- ½ teaspoon lime zest, grated
- A pinch of salt and black pepper
- ¼ cup dill, chopped

DIRECTIONS:

1. In a salad bowl, mix the avocados with the tomatoes and the rest of the ingredients, toss, and serve cold.

NUTRITION: Calories: 188 Fat: 7.3g Fiber: 4.9g Carbs: 6.4g Protein: 6.5g

Summer Vegetables

Preparation time: 20 minutes.
Level: Difficult.
Cooking time: 1 hour 40 minutes.
Servings: 4
INGREDIENTS:

- 1 teaspoon dried marjoram
- 1/3 cup Parmesan cheese
- 1 small eggplant, sliced into ¼-inch thick circles
- 1 small summer squash, peeled and sliced diagonally into a ¼-inch thickness
- 3 large tomatoes, sliced into ¼-inch thick circles
- ½ cup dry white wine
- ½ teaspoon freshly ground pepper, divided
- ½ teaspoon salt, divided
- 5 cloves garlic, sliced thinly
- 2 cups leeks, sliced thinly
- 4 tablespoons extra-virgin olive oil, divided

DIRECTIONS:

1. On medium fire, place a large nonstick saucepan and heat 2 tablespoons of oil.
2. Sauté garlic and leeks for 6 minutes or until garlic is starting to brown. Season with pepper and salt, ¼ teaspoon each.
3. Pour in the wine and cook for another minute. Transfer to a 2-quart baking dish.
4. In a baking dish, layer in an alternating pattern the eggplant, summer squash, and tomatoes. Do this until the dish is covered with vegetables. If there are excess vegetables, store them for future use.
5. Season with the remaining pepper and salt. Drizzle with the remaining olive oil and pop in a preheated 425°F oven.
6. Bake for 75 minutes. Remove from the oven and top with marjoram and cheese.
7. Return to oven and bake for 15 minutes more or until veggies are soft and edges are browned.
8. Allow cooling for at least 5 minutes before serving.

NUTRITION: Calories: 150 Carbs: 11.8g Protein: 3.3g Fat: 10.8g

Beans and Cucumber Salad

Preparation time: 10 minutes.
Level: Easy.
Cooking time: 0 minutes.
Servings: 4
INGREDIENTS:

- 15 ounces canned great northern beans, drained and rinsed
- 2 tablespoons olive oil
- ½ cup baby arugula
- 1 cup cucumber, sliced
- 1 tablespoon parsley, chopped
- 2 tomatoes, cubed
- A pinch of sea salt and black pepper
- 2 tablespoons balsamic vinegar

DIRECTIONS:

1. In a bowl, mix the beans with the cucumber and the rest of the ingredients, toss and serve cold.

NUTRITION: Calories: 233 Fat: 9g Fiber: 6.5g Carbs: 13g Protein: 8g

Minty Olives and Tomatoes Salad

Preparation time: 10 minutes.
Level: Easy.
Cooking time: 0 minutes.
Servings: 4
INGREDIENTS:

- 1 cup kalamata olives, pitted and sliced
- 1 cup black olives, pitted and halved
- 1 cup cherry tomatoes, halved
- 4 tomatoes, chopped
- 1 red onion, chopped
- 2 tablespoons oregano, chopped
- 1 tablespoon mint, chopped
- 2 tablespoons balsamic vinegar
- ¼ cup olive oil
- 2 teaspoons Italian herbs, dried
- A pinch of sea salt and black pepper

DIRECTIONS:

1. In a salad bowl, mix the olives with the tomatoes and the rest of the ingredients, toss, and serve cold.

NUTRITION: Calories: 190 Fat: 8.1g Fiber: 5.8g Carbs: 11.6g Protein: 4.6g

Summer Veggies in Instant Pot

Preparation time: 10 minutes.
Level: Easy.
Cooking time: 7 minutes.
Servings: 4
INGREDIENTS:

- 2 cups okra, sliced
- 1 cup grape tomatoes
- 1 cup mushroom, sliced
- 1(½) cups onion, sliced
- 2 cups bell pepper, sliced
- 2(½) cups zucchini, sliced
- 2 tablespoons basil, chopped
- 1 tablespoon thyme, chopped
- ½ cups balsamic vinegar
- ½ cups olive oil
- Salt and pepper to taste

DIRECTIONS:

1. Place all the ingredients in the Instant Pot.
2. Stir the contents and close the lid.
3. Close the lid and press the Manual button.
4. Adjust the cooking time to 7 minutes.
5. Do quick pressure release.
6. Once cooled, evenly divide into serving size, keep in your preferred container, and refrigerate until ready to eat.

NUTRITION: Calories: 233 Carbs: 7g Protein: 3g Fat: 18g

Sumptuous Tomato Soup

Preparation time: 10 minutes.
Level: Average.
Cooking time: 30 minutes.
Servings: 4
INGREDIENTS:

- Pepper and salt to taste
- 2 tablespoons tomato paste
- 1(½) cups vegetable broth
- 1 tablespoon chopped parsley
- 1 tablespoon olive oil
- 5 garlic cloves
- ½ medium yellow onion
- 4 large ripe tomatoes

DIRECTIONS:

1. Preheat the oven to 350°F.
2. Chop onion and tomatoes into thin wedges. Place on a rimmed baking sheet. Season with parsley, pepper, salt, and olive oil. Toss to combine well. Hide the garlic cloves inside tomatoes to keep them from burning.
3. Pop in the oven and bake for 30 minutes.
4. On medium pot, bring vegetable stock to a simmer. Add tomato paste.
5. Pour baked tomato mixture into the pot. Continue simmering for another 10 minutes.
6. With an immersion blender, puree soup.
7. Adjust salt and pepper to taste before serving.

NUTRITION: Calories: 179 Carbs: 26.7g Protein: 5.2g Fat: 7.7g

Superfast Cajun Asparagus

Preparation time: 10 minutes.
Level: Easy
Cooking time: 8 minutes.
Servings: 4
INGREDIENTS:

- 1 pound asparagus

DIRECTIONS:

1. Snap the asparagus and make sure that you use the tender part of the vegetable.
2. Place a large skillet on the stovetop and heat on high for a minute.
3. Then grease skillet with cooking spray and spread asparagus in one layer.
4. Cover skillet and continue cooking on high for 5 to eight minutes.
5. Halfway through cooking time, stir the skillet and then cover and continue to cook.
6. Once done cooking, transfer to plates, serve, and enjoy!

NUTRITION: Calories: 81 Carbs: 0g Protein: 0g Fat: 9g

Sweet and Nutritious Pumpkin Soup

Preparation time: 20 minutes.
Level: Difficult.
Cooking time: 40 minutes.
Servings: 4
INGREDIENTS:

- 1 teaspoon chopped fresh parsley
- ½ cup half and half
- ½ teaspoon chopped fresh thyme
- 1 teaspoon salt
- 4 cups pumpkin puree
- 6 cups vegetable stock, divided
- 1 clove garlic, minced
- 1(1-inch) piece ginger root, peeled and minced
- 1 cup chopped onion

DIRECTIONS:

1. On medium-high fire, place a heavy-bottomed pot and for 5 minutes heat ½ cup vegetable stock, ginger, garlic, and onions. Cook until veggies are tender.
2. Add the remaining stock and cook for 30 minutes.
3. Season with thyme and salt.
4. With an immersion blender, puree soup until smooth.
5. Turn off the fire and mix in half and half.
6. Transfer pumpkin soup into 8 bowls, garnish with parsley, serve and enjoy.

NUTRITION: Calories: 58 Carbs: 6.6g Protein: 5.1g Fat: 1.7g

Sweet Potato Puree

Preparation time: 10 minutes.
Level: Easy.
Cooking time: 15 minutes.
Servings: 4
INGREDIENTS:

- 2 pounds sweet potatoes, peeled
- 1(½) cups water
- 5 Medjool dates, pitted and chopped

DIRECTIONS:

1. Place all the ingredients in a pot.
2. Close the lid and allow boiling for 15 minutes until the potatoes are soft.
3. Drain the potatoes and place them in a food processor together with the dates.
4. Pulse until smooth.
5. Place in individual containers.
6. Put a label and store it in the fridge.
7. Allow thawing at room temperature before heating in the microwave oven.

NUTRITION: Calories: 619 Carbs: 97.8g Protein: 4.8g Fat: 24.3g

Sweet Potatoes Oven Fried

Preparation time: 10 minutes.
Level: Average.
Cooking time: 30 minutes.
Servings: 4
INGREDIENTS:

- 1 small garlic clove, minced
- 1 teaspoon grated orange rind
- 1 tablespoon fresh parsley, chopped finely
- ¼ teaspoon pepper
- ¼ teaspoon salt
- 1 tablespoon olive oil
- 4 medium sweet potatoes, peeled and sliced into a ¼-inch thickness

DIRECTIONS:

1. In a large bowl mix well pepper, salt, olive oil, and sweet potatoes.
2. In a greased baking sheet, in a single layer arrange sweet potatoes.
3. Pop in a preheated 400°F oven and bake for 15 minutes, turnover potato slices, and return to oven. Bake for another 15 minutes or until tender.
4. Meanwhile, mix well in a small bowl, garlic, orange rind, and parsley, sprinkle over cooked potato slices, and serve.
5. You can store baked sweet potatoes in a lidded container and just microwave whenever you want to eat them. Consume within 3 days.

NUTRITION: Calories: 176 Carbs: 36.6g Protein: 2.5g Fat: 2.5g

Tasty Avocado Sauce over Zoodles

Preparation time: 10 minutes.
Level: Easy.
Cooking time: 10 minutes.
Servings: 4
INGREDIENTS:

- 1 zucchini peeled and spiralized into noodles
- 4 tablespoons pine nuts
- 2 tablespoons lemon juice
- 1 avocado peeled and pitted
- 12 sliced cherry tomatoes
- 1/3 cup water
- 1(1/4) cup basil
- Pepper and salt to taste

DIRECTIONS:

1. Make the sauce in a blender by adding pine nuts, lemon juice, avocado, water, and basil. Pulse until smooth and creamy. Season with pepper and salt to taste. Mix well.
2. Place zoodles in the salad bowl. Pour over the avocado sauce and toss well to coat.
3. Add cherry tomatoes, serve, and enjoy.

NUTRITION: Calories: 313 Protein: 6.8g Carbs: 18.7g Fat: 26.8g

Tomato Basil Cauliflower Rice

Preparation time: 5 minutes.
Level: Easy.
Cooking time: 10 minutes.
Servings: 4
INGREDIENTS:

- Salt and pepper to taste
- Dried parsley for garnish
- ¼ cup tomato paste
- ½ teaspoon garlic, minced
- ½ teaspoon onion powder
- ½ teaspoon marjoram
- 1(½) teaspoon dried basil
- 1 teaspoon dried oregano
- 1 large head of cauliflower
- 1 teaspoon oil

DIRECTIONS:

1. Cut the cauliflower into florets and place it in the food processor.
2. Pulse until it has a coarse consistency similar to rice. Set aside.
3. In a skillet, heat the oil and sauté the garlic and onion for three minutes. Add the rest of the ingredients. Cook for 8 minutes.

NUTRITION: Calories: 106 Carbs: 15.1g Protein: 3.3g Fat: 5.0g

Vegan Sesame Tofu and Eggplants

Preparation time: 10 minutes.
Level: Average.
Cooking time: 20 minutes.
Servings: 4
INGREDIENTS:

- 5 tablespoons olive oil
- 1 pound firm tofu, sliced
- 3 tablespoons rice vinegar
- 2 teaspoons Swerve sweetener
- 2 whole eggplants, sliced
- ¼ cup soy sauce
- Salt and pepper to taste
- 4 tablespoons toasted sesame oil
- ¼ cup sesame seeds
- 1 cup fresh cilantro, chopped

DIRECTIONS:

1. Heat the oil in a pan for 2 minutes.
2. Pan-fry the tofu for 3 minutes on each side.
3. Stir in the rice vinegar, sweetener, eggplants, and soy sauce. Season with salt and pepper to taste.
4. Cover and cook for 5 minutes on medium fire. Stir and continue cooking for another 5 minutes.
5. Toss in the sesame oil, sesame seeds, and cilantro.
6. Serve and enjoy.

NUTRITION: Calories: 616 Carbs: 27.4g Protein: 23.9g Fat: 49.2g

Vegetarian Coconut Curry

Preparation time: 10 minutes.
Level: Average.
Cooking time: 30 minutes.
Servings: 4
INGREDIENTS:

- 4 tablespoons coconut oil
- 1 medium onion, chopped
- 1 teaspoon minced garlic
- 1 teaspoon minced ginger
- 1 cup broccoli florets
- 2 cups fresh spinach leaves
- 2 teaspoons fish sauce
- 1 tablespoon garam masala
- ½ cup coconut milk
- Salt and pepper to taste

DIRECTIONS:

1. Heat oil in a pot.
2. Sauté the onion and garlic until fragrant, around 3 minutes.
3. Stir in the rest of the ingredients, except for spinach leaves.
4. Season with salt and pepper to taste.
5. Cover and cook on medium fire for 5 minutes.
6. Stir and add spinach leaves. Cover and cook for another 2 minutes.
7. Turn off the fire and let it sit for two more minutes before serving.

NUTRITION: Calories: 210 Carbs: 6.5g Protein: 2.1g Fat: 20.9g

Vegetable Soup Moroccan Style

Preparation time: 10 minutes.
Level: Easy.
Cooking time: 10 minutes.
Servings: 4
INGREDIENTS:

- ½ teaspoon pepper
- 1 teaspoon salt
- 2 ounces whole-wheat orzo
- 1 large zucchini, peeled, and cut into ¼-inch cubes
- 8 sprigs of fresh cilantro, plus more leaves for garnish
- 12 sprigs flat-leaf parsley, plus more for garnish
- A pinch of saffron threads
- 2 stalks celery leaves included, sliced thinly
- 2 carrots, diced
- 2 small turnips, peeled and diced
- 1(14-ounces) can dice tomatoes
- 6 cups water
- 1 pound lamb stew meat, trimmed and cut into ½-inch cubes
- 2 teaspoons ground turmeric
- 1 medium onion, diced finely
- 2 tablespoons extra-virgin olive oil

DIRECTIONS:

1. On medium-high fire, place a large Dutch oven and heat oil.
2. Add turmeric and onion, stir-fry for two minutes.
3. Add meat and sauté for 5 minutes.
4. Add saffron, celery, carrots, turnips, tomatoes and juice, and water.
5. With a kitchen string, tie cilantro and parsley sprigs together and into the pot.
6. Cover and bring to a boil. Once boiling, reduce fire to a simmer and continue to cook for 45 to 50 minutes or until meat is tender.
7. Once the meat is tender, stir in zucchini. Cover and cook for 8 minutes.
8. Add orzo; cook for 10 minutes or until soft.
9. Remove and discard cilantro and parsley sprigs.
10. Season with pepper and salt.
11. Transfer to a serving bowl and garnish with cilantro and parsley leaves before serving.

NUTRITION: Calories: 268 Carbs: 12.9g Protein: 28.1g Fat: 11.7g

Yummy Cauliflower Fritters

Preparation time: 10 minutes.
Level: Easy.
Cooking time: 15 minutes.
Servings: 4
INGREDIENTS:

- 1 large cauliflower head, cut into florets
- 2 eggs, beaten
- ½ teaspoon turmeric
- ½ teaspoon salt
- ¼ teaspoon black pepper
- 6 tablespoons coconut oil

DIRECTIONS:

1. Place the cauliflower florets in a pot with water.
2. Bring to a boil and drain once cooked.
3. Place the cauliflower, eggs, turmeric, salt, and pepper into the food processor.
4. Pulse until the mixture becomes coarse.
5. Transfer into a bowl. Using your hands, form six small flattened balls and place them in the fridge for at least 1 hour until the mixture hardens.
6. Heat the oil in a skillet and fry the cauliflower patties for 3 minutes on each side
7. Place in individual containers.
8. Put a label and store it in the fridge.
9. Allow thawing at room temperature before heating in the microwave oven.

NUTRITION: Calories: 157 Carbs: 2.8g Protein: 3.9g Fat: 15.3g Fiber: 0.9g

Zucchini Garlic Fries

Preparation time: 15 minutes.
Level: Average.
Cooking time: 20 minutes.
Servings: 4
INGREDIENTS:

- ¼ teaspoon garlic powder
- ½ cup almond flour
- 2 large egg whites, beaten
- 3 medium zucchinis, sliced into fry sticks
- Salt and pepper to taste

DIRECTIONS:

1. Preheat the oven to 400°F.
2. Mix all the ingredients in a bowl until the zucchini fries are well coated.
3. Place fries on the cookie sheet and spread evenly.
4. Put in the oven and cook for 20 minutes.
5. Halfway through cooking time, stir-fries.

NUTRITION: Calories: 11 Carbs: 1.1g Protein: 1.5g Fat: 0.1g

Zucchini Pasta with Mango-Kiwi Sauce

Preparation time: 5 minutes.
Level: Average.
Cooking time: 20 minutes.
Servings: 4
INGREDIENTS:

- 1 teaspoon dried herbs, optional
- ½ cup raw kale leaves, shredded
- 2 small dried figs
- 3 Medjool dates
- 4 medium kiwis
- 2 big mangos, seed discarded
- 2 cup zucchini, spiralized
- ¼ cup roasted cashew

Directions:

1. On a salad bowl, place kale then topped with zucchini noodles and sprinkle with dried herbs. Set aside.
2. In a food processor, grind to a powder the cashews. Add figs, dates, kiwis, and mangoes then puree to a smooth consistency. Pour over zucchini pasta, serve and enjoy.

Nutrition: Calories: 530 Carbs: 95.4g Protein: 8.0g Fat: 18.5g

Quinoa with Almonds and Cranberries

Preparation time: 10 minutes.
Level: Easy.
Cooking time: 15 minutes.
Servings: 4
INGREDIENTS:

- 2 cups cooked quinoa
- 1/3 teaspoon cranberries or currants
- ¼ cup sliced almonds
- 2 garlic cloves, minced
- 1(¼) teaspoon salt
- ½ teaspoon ground cumin
- ½ teaspoon turmeric
- ¼ teaspoon ground cinnamon
- ¼ teaspoon freshly ground black pepper

DIRECTIONS:

1. In a large bowl, toss the quinoa, cranberries, almonds, garlic, salt, cumin, turmeric, cinnamon, and pepper and stir to combine. Enjoy alone or with roasted cauliflower.

NUTRITION: Calories: 430 Carbs: 65.4g Protein: 8.0g Fat: 15.5g

Mediterranean Baked Chickpeas

Preparation time: 15 minutes.
Level: Easy.
Cooking time: 15 minutes.
Servings: 4
INGREDIENTS:

- 1 tablespoon extra-virgin olive oil
- ½ medium onion, chopped
- 3 garlic cloves, chopped
- 2 teaspoons smoked paprika
- ¼ teaspoon ground cumin
- 4 cups halved cherry tomatoes
- 2 (15-ounces) cans chickpeas, drained and rinsed
- ½ cup plain, unsweetened, full-fat Greek yogurt, for serving
- 1 cup crumbled feta, for serving

DIRECTIONS:

1. Preheat the oven to 425°F.
2. In an oven-safe sauté pan or skillet, heat the oil over medium heat and sauté the onion and garlic. Cook for about 5 minutes, until softened and fragrant. Stir in the paprika and cumin and cook for 2 minutes. Stir in the tomatoes and chickpeas.
3. Bring to a simmer for 5 to 10 minutes before placing in the oven.
4. Roast in the oven for 25 to 30 minutes, until bubbling and thickened. To serve, top with Greek yogurt and feta.

NUTRITION: Calories: 330 Carbs: 75.4g Protein: 9.0g Fat: 18.5g

Falafel Bites

Preparation time: 10 minutes.
Level: Easy.
Cooking time: 15 minutes.
Servings: 4
INGREDIENTS:

- 1(2/3) cups falafel mix
- 1(¼) cups water
- Extra-virgin olive oil spray
- 1 tablespoon pickled onions (optional)
- 1 tablespoon pickled turnips (optional)
- 2 tablespoons tzatziki sauce (optional)

DIRECTIONS:

1. In a large bowl, carefully stir the falafel mix into the water. Mix well. Let stand 15 minutes to absorb the water. Form the mix into 1-inch balls and arrange on a baking sheet.
2. Preheat the broiler to high.
3. Take the balls and flatten them slightly with your thumb (so they won't roll around on the baking sheet). Spray with olive oil, and then broil for 2 to 3 minutes on each side, until crispy and brown.
4. To fry the falafel, fill a pot with ½ inch of cooking oil and heat over medium-high heat to 375°F. Fry the balls for about 3 minutes, until brown and crisp. Drain on paper towels and serve with pickled onions, pickled turnips, and tzatziki sauce (if using).

NUTRITION: Calories: 530 Carbs: 95.4g Protein: 8.0g Fat: 18.5g

Quick Vegetable Kebabs

Preparation time: 15 minutes.
Level: Average.
Cooking time: 20 minutes.
Servings: 4
INGREDIENTS:

- 4 medium red onions, peeled and sliced into 6 wedges
- 4 medium zucchinis, cut into 1-inch-thick slices
- 4 bell peppers, cut into 2-inch squares
- 2 yellow bell peppers, cut into 2-inch squares
- 2 orange bell peppers, cut into 2-inch squares
- 2 beefsteak tomatoes, cut into quarters
- 3 tablespoons herbed oil

DIRECTIONS:

1. Preheat the oven or grill to medium-high or 350°F.
2. Thread 1-piece red onion, zucchini, different colored bell peppers, and tomatoes onto a skewer. Repeat until the skewer is full of vegetables, up to 2 inches away from the skewer end, and continue until all skewers are complete.
3. Put the skewers on a baking sheet and cook in the oven for 10 minutes or grill for 5 minutes on each side. The vegetables will be done with they reach your desired crunch or softness.
4. Remove the skewers from heat and drizzle with herbed oil.

NUTRITION: Calories: 235 Carbs: 30.4g Protein: 8.0g Fat: 14.5g

Tortellini in Red Pepper Sauce

Preparation time: 15 minutes.
Level: Easy.
Cooking time: 10 minutes.
Servings: 4
INGREDIENTS:

- 1(16-ounces) container fresh cheese tortellini (usually green and white pasta)
- 1(16-ounces) jar roasted red peppers, drained
- 1 teaspoon garlic powder
- ¼ cup tahini
- 1 tablespoon red pepper oil (optional)

DIRECTIONS:

1. Bring a large pot of water to a boil and cook the tortellini according to package directions.
2. In a blender, combine the red peppers with the garlic powder and process until smooth. Once blended, add the tahini until the sauce is thickened. If the sauce gets too thick, add up to 1 tablespoon of red pepper oil (if using).
3. Once tortellini is cooked, drain and leave the pasta in a colander. Add the sauce to the bottom of the empty pot and heat for 2 minutes. Then, add the tortellini back into the pot and cook for 2 more minutes. Serve and enjoy!

NUTRITION: Calories: 530 Carbs: 95.4g Protein: 8.0g Fat: 18.5g

Freekeh, Chickpea, and Herb Salad

Preparation time: 15 minutes.
Level: Easy.
Cooking time: 10 minutes.
Servings: 4
INGREDIENTS:

- 1(15-ounces) can chickpeas, rinsed and drained
- 1 cup cooked freekeh
- 1 cup thinly sliced celery
- 1 bunch scallions, both white and green parts, finely chopped
- ½ cup chopped fresh flat-leaf parsley
- ¼ cup chopped fresh mint
- 3 tablespoons chopped celery leaves
- ½ teaspoon kosher salt
- 1/3 cup extra-virgin olive oil
- ¼ cup freshly squeezed lemon juice
- ¼ teaspoon cumin seeds
- 1 teaspoon garlic powder

DIRECTIONS:

1. In a large bowl, combine the chickpeas, freekeh, celery, scallions, parsley, mint, celery leaves, and salt and toss lightly.
2. In a small bowl, whisk together the olive oil, lemon juice, cumin seeds, and garlic powder. Once combined, add to freekeh salad.

NUTRITION: Calories: 230 Carbs: 25.4g Protein: 8.0g Fat: 18.5g

Creamy Chickpea Sauce with Whole-Wheat Fusilli

Preparation time: 15 minutes.
Level: Average.
Cooking time: 20 minutes.
Servings: 4
INGREDIENTS:

- ¼ cup extra-virgin olive oil
- ½ large shallot, chopped
- 5 garlic cloves, thinly sliced
- 1(15-ounces) can chickpeas, drained and rinsed, reserving ½ cup canning liquid
- Pinch red pepper flakes
- 1 cup whole-grain fusilli pasta
- ¼ teaspoon salt
- 1/8 teaspoon freshly ground black pepper
- ¼ cup shaved fresh Parmesan cheese
- ¼ cup chopped fresh basil
- 2 teaspoons dried parsley
- 1 teaspoon dried oregano

DIRECTIONS:

1. In a medium pan, heat the oil over medium heat, and sauté the shallot and garlic for 3 to 5 minutes, until the garlic is golden. Add ¾ of the chickpeas plus 2 tablespoons of liquid from the can and bring to a simmer.
2. Remove from the heat, transfer into a standard blender, and blend until smooth. At this point, add the remaining chickpeas. Add more reserved chickpea liquid if it becomes thick.
3. Bring a large pot of salted water to a boil and cook pasta until al dente about 8 minutes. Reserve ½ cup of the pasta water, drain the pasta, and return it to the pot.
4. Add the chickpea sauce to the hot pasta and add up to ¼ cup of the pasta water. You may need to add more pasta water to reach your desired consistency.
5. Place the pasta pot over medium heat and mix occasionally until the sauce thickens. Season with salt and pepper.
6. Serve, garnished with Parmesan, basil, parsley, oregano, and red pepper flakes.

NUTRITION: Calories: 230 Carbs: 20.4g Protein: 8.0g Fat: 18.5g

Peppers and Lentils Salad

Preparation time: 10 minutes.
Level: Easy.
Cooking time: 0 minutes.
Servings: 4
INGREDIENTS:

- 14 ounces canned lentils, drained and rinsed
- 2 spring onions, chopped
- 1 red bell pepper, chopped
- 1 green bell pepper, chopped
- 1 tablespoon fresh lime juice
- 1/3 cup coriander, chopped
- 2 teaspoons balsamic vinegar

DIRECTIONS:

1. In a salad bowl, combine the lentils with the onions, bell peppers, and the rest of the ingredients, toss and serve.

NUTRITION: Calories: 200 Fat: 2.45g Fiber: 6.7g Carbs: 10.5g Protein: 5.6g

Cashews and Red Cabbage Salad

Preparation time: 10 minutes.
Level: Easy.
Cooking time: 0 minutes.
Servings: 4
INGREDIENTS:
- 1 pound red cabbage, shredded
- 2 tablespoons coriander, chopped
- ½ cup cashews, halved
- 2 tablespoons olive oil
- 1 tomato, cubed
- A pinch of salt and black pepper
- 1 tablespoon white vinegar

DIRECTIONS:
1. In a salad bowl, combine the cabbage with the coriander and the rest of the ingredients, toss, and serve cold.

NUTRITION: Calories: 210 Fat: 6.3g Fiber: 5.2g Carbs: 5.5g Protein: 8g

Apples and Pomegranate Salad

Preparation time: 10 minutes.
Level: Easy.
Cooking time: 0 minutes.
Servings: 4
INGREDIENTS:

- 3 big apples, cored and cubed
- 1 cup pomegranate seeds
- 3 cups baby arugula
- 1 cup walnuts, chopped
- 1 tablespoon olive oil
- 1 teaspoon white sesame seeds
- 2 tablespoons apple cider vinegar
- Salt and black pepper to taste

DIRECTIONS:

1. In a bowl, mix the apples with the arugula and the rest of the ingredients, toss, and serve cold.

NUTRITION: Calories: 160 Fat: 4.3g Fiber: 5.3g Carbs: 8.7g Protein: 10g

Cranberry Bulgur Mix

Preparation time: 10 minutes.
Level: Easy.
Cooking time: 0 minutes.
Servings: 4
INGREDIENTS:

- 1(½) cups hot water
- 1 cup bulgur
- Juice of ½ lemon
- 4 tablespoons cilantro, chopped
- ½ cup cranberries, chopped
- 1(½) teaspoons curry powder
- ¼ cup green onions, chopped
- ½ cup red bell peppers, chopped
- ½ cup carrots, grated
- 1 tablespoon olive oil
- A pinch of salt and black pepper

DIRECTIONS:

1. Put bulgur into a bowl, add the water, stir, cover, and leave aside for 10 minutes, fluff with a fork, and transfer to a bowl.
2. Add the rest of the ingredients, toss, and serve cold.

NUTRITION: Calories: 300 Fat: 6.4g Fiber: 6.1g Carbs: 7.6g Protein: 13g

Chickpeas, Corn, and Black Beans Salad

Preparation time: 10 minutes.
Level: Easy.
Cooking time: 0 minutes.
Servings: 4
INGREDIENTS:

- 1(½) cups canned black beans, drained and rinsed
- ½ teaspoon garlic powder
- 2 teaspoons chili powder
- A pinch of sea salt and black pepper
- 1(½) cups canned chickpeas, drained and rinsed
- 1 cup baby spinach
- 1 avocado, pitted, peeled, and chopped
- 1 cup corn kernels, chopped
- 2 tablespoons lemon juice
- 1 tablespoon olive oil
- 1 tablespoon apple cider vinegar
- 1 teaspoon chives, chopped

DIRECTIONS:

1. In a salad bowl, combine the black beans with the garlic powder, chili powder, and the rest of the ingredients, toss, and serve cold.

NUTRITION: Calories: 300 Fat: 13.4g Fiber: 4.1g Carbs: 8.6g Protein: 13g

Olives and Lentils Salad

Preparation time: 10 minutes.
Level: Easy.
Cooking time: 0 minutes.
Servings: 4
INGREDIENTS:

- 1/3 cup canned green lentils, drained and rinsed
- 1 tablespoon olive oil
- 2 cups baby spinach
- 1 cup black olives, pitted and halved
- 2 tablespoons sunflower seeds
- 1 tablespoon Dijon mustard
- 2 tablespoons balsamic vinegar
- 2 tablespoons olive oil

DIRECTIONS:

1. In a bowl, mix the lentils with the spinach, olives, and the rest of the ingredients, toss and serve cold.

NUTRITION: Calories: 279 Fat: 6.5g Fiber: 4.5g Carbs: 9.6g Protein: 12g

Lime Spinach and Chickpeas Salad

Preparation time: 10 minutes.
Level: Easy.
Cooking time: 0 minutes.
Servings: 4
INGREDIENTS:

- 16 ounces canned chickpeas, drained and rinsed
- 2 cups baby spinach leaves
- ½ tablespoon lime juice
- 2 tablespoons olive oil
- 1 teaspoon cumin, ground
- A pinch of sea salt and black pepper
- ½ teaspoon chili flakes

DIRECTIONS:

1. In a bowl, mix the chickpeas with the spinach and the rest of the ingredients, toss, and serve cold.

NUTRITION: Calories: 240 Fat: 8.2g Fiber: 5.3g Carbs: 11.6g Protein: 12g

Whipped Potatoes

Preparation time: 20 minutes.
Level: Average.
Cooking time: 35 minutes.
Servings: 4
INGREDIENTS:

- 4 cups water
- 3 pounds potatoes, sliced into cubes
- 3 cloves garlic, crushed
- 6 tablespoons butter
- 10 sage leaves
- ½ cup Greek yogurt
- ¼ cup low-fat milk

DIRECTION:

1. Cook potatoes in water for 30 minutes. Drain. Cook garlic in butter for 1 minute over medium heat. Add the sage and cook for 5 more minutes. Discard the garlic. Use a fork to mash the potatoes.
2. Whip using an electric mixer while gradually adding the butter, yogurt, and milk. Season with salt.

NUTRITION: Calories: 169 Carbohydrates: 22g Protein: 4.2g

Jalapeno Rice Noodles

Preparation time: 10 minutes.
Level: Average.
Cooking time: 25 minutes.
Servings: 4
INGREDIENTS

- ¼ cup soy sauce
- 1 tablespoon brown sugar
- 2 teaspoons sriracha
- 3 tablespoons lime juice
- 8 ounces rice noodles
- 3 teaspoons toasted sesame oil
- 1 package extra-firm tofu, pressed
- 1 onion, sliced
- 2 cups green cabbage, shredded
- 1 small jalapeno, minced
- 1 red bell pepper, sliced
- 1 yellow bell pepper, sliced
- 3 garlic cloves, minced
- 3 scallions, sliced
- 1 cup Thai basil leaves, roughly chopped
- Lime wedges for serving

DIRECTIONS:

1. Fill a suitably-sized pot with salted water and boil it on high heat.
2. Add pasta to the boiling water and cook until it is al dente, then rinse under cold water.
3. Put the lime juice, soy sauce, sriracha, and brown sugar in a bowl then mix well.
4. Place a large wok over medium heat then add 1 teaspoon of sesame oil.
5. Toss in tofu and stir for 5 minutes until golden brown.
6. Transfer the golden-brown tofu to a plate and add 2 teaspoons of oil to the wok.
7. Stir in scallions, garlic, peppers, cabbage, and onion.
8. Sauté for 2 minutes, then add cooked noodles and prepared sauce.
9. Cook for 2 minutes, then garnish with lime wedges and basil leaves.
10. Serve fresh.

NUTRITION: Calories: 45 Fat: 2.5g Protein: 4g Carbohydrates: 9g Fiber: 4g Sugar: 3g Sodium: 20mg

Sautéed Cabbage

Preparation time: 8 minutes.
Level: Easy.
Cooking time: 12 minutes.
Servings: 4

INGREDIENTS:

- ¼ cup butter
- 1 onion, sliced thinly
- 1 head cabbage, sliced into wedges
- Salt and pepper to taste
- Crumbled crispy bacon bits for serving

DIRECTIONS:

1. Add the butter to a pan over medium-high heat. Cook the onion for 1 minute, stirring frequently. Season with salt and pepper. Add the cabbage and cook while stirring for 12 minutes. Sprinkle with the crispy bacon bits.

NUTRITION: Calories: 77 Fat: 5.9g Saturated fat: 3.6g Carbohydrates: 6.1g Fiber: 2.4g Protein: 1.3g

Curry Apple Couscous with Leeks and Pecans

Preparation time: 15 minutes.
Level: Easy.
Cooking time: 8 minutes.
Servings: 4
INGREDIENTS:

- 2 teaspoons extra-virgin olive oil
- 2 leeks, white parts only, sliced
- 1 apple, diced
- 2 cups cooked couscous
- 2 tablespoons curry powder
- ½ cup chopped pecans

DIRECTIONS:

1. Heat the olive oil in a skillet over medium heat until shimmering. Add the leeks and sauté for 5 minutes or until soft.
2. Add the diced apple and cook for 3 more minutes until tender. Add the couscous and curry powder. Stir to combine. Transfer them in a large serving bowl, then mix in the pecans and serve.

NUTRITION: Calories: 254 Fat: 11.9g Protein: 5.4g Carbs: 34.3g

Farro Salad Mix

Preparation time: 15 minutes.
Level: Average.
Cooking time: 33 minutes.
Servings: 4
INGREDIENTS:

- 1 teaspoon Dijon mustard
- 1(½) cups whole farro
- 2 ounces feta cheese, crumbled (½ cup)
- 2 tablespoons lemon juice
- 2 tablespoons minced shallot
- 3 tablespoons chopped fresh dill
- 3 tablespoons extra-virgin olive oil
- 6 ounces asparagus, trimmed and cut into 1-inch lengths
- 6 ounces cherry tomatoes, halved
- 6 ounces sugar snap peas, strings removed, cut into 1-inch lengths
- Salt and pepper to taste

DIRECTIONS:

1. Bring 4 quarts of water to boil in a Dutch oven. Put in asparagus, snap peas, and 1 tablespoon salt and cook until crisp-tender, approximately 3 minutes.
2. Use a slotted spoon to move vegetables to a large plate and allow them to cool completely for about 15 minutes. Put in farro to water, return to boil, and cook until grains are soft with a slight chew, 15 to 30 minutes.
3. Drain farro, spread in rimmed baking sheet, and allow cooling completely for about 15 minutes.
4. Beat oil, lemon juice, shallot, mustard, ¼ teaspoon salt, and ¼ teaspoon pepper together in a big container.
5. Put in vegetables, farro, tomatoes, dill, and ¼ cup feta and toss gently to combine. Sprinkle with salt and pepper to taste. Move to a serving platter and drizzle with the remaining ¼ cup feta. Serve.

NUTRITION: Calories: 240 Carbs: 26g Fat: 12g Protein: 9g

Lemony Farro and Avocado Bowl

Preparation time: 15 minutes.
Level: Average.
Cooking time: 25 minutes.
Servings: 4
INGREDIENTS:

- 1 tablespoon plus 2 teaspoons extra-virgin olive oil, divided
- ½ medium onion, chopped
- 1 carrot, shredded
- 2 garlic cloves, minced
- 1 (6-ounces/170-grams) cup pearled farro
- 2 cups low-sodium vegetable soup
- 2 avocados, peeled, pitted, and sliced
- Zest and juice of 1 small lemon
- ¼ teaspoon sea salt

DIRECTIONS:

1. Heat 1 tablespoon of olive oil in a saucepan over medium-high heat until shimmering. Add the onion and sauté for 5 minutes or until translucent. Add the carrot and garlic and sauté for 1 minute or until fragrant.
2. Add the farro and pour in the vegetable soup. Bring to a boil over high heat. Reduce the heat to low. Put the lid on and simmer for 20 minutes or until the farro is al dente.
3. Transfer the farro to a large serving bowl, then fold in the avocado slices. Sprinkle with lemon zest and salt, then drizzle with lemon juice and 2 teaspoons of olive oil. Stir to mix well and serve immediately.

NUTRITION: Calories: 210 Fat: 11.1g Protein: 4.2g Carbs: 27.9g

Chapter 8:
FISH AND SEAFOOD RECIPES

Baked Cod Fillets with Ghee Sauce

Preparation time: 10 minutes.
Level: Easy.
Cooking time: 15 minutes.
Servings: 4
INGREDIENTS:

- Pepper and salt to taste
- 2 tablespoons minced parsley
- 1 lemon, sliced into ¼-inch thick circles
- 1 lemon, juiced, and peeled
- 4 garlic cloves, crushed, peeled, and minced
- ¼ cup melted ghee
- 4 cod fillets

DIRECTIONS:

1. Bring oven to 425°F.
2. Mix parsley, lemon juice, lemon zest, garlic, and melted ghee in a small bowl. Mix well and then season with pepper and salt to taste.
3. Prepare a large baking dish by greasing it with cooking spray.
4. Evenly lay the cod fillets on the greased dish. Season generously with pepper and salt.
5. Pour the bowl of garlic-ghee sauce from step 2 on top of cod fillets. Top the cod fillets with the thinly sliced lemon.
6. Pop in the preheated oven and bake until flaky, around 13 to 15 minutes. Remove from the oven, transfer to dishes, serve, and enjoy.

NUTRITION: Calories: 200 Fat: 12g Protein: 21g Carbs: 2g

Avocado Peach Salsa on Grilled Swordfish

Preparation time: 15 minutes.
Level: Easy.
Cooking time: 12 minutes.
Servings: 4
INGREDIENTS:

- 1 garlic clove, minced
- 1 lemon juice
- 1 tablespoon apple cider vinegar
- 1 tablespoon coconut oil
- 1 teaspoon honey
- 2 swordfish fillets (around 4oz each)
- Pinch cayenne pepper
- Pinch of pepper and salt

Salsa ingredients:

- ¼ red onion, finely chopped
- ½ cup cilantro, finely chopped
- 1 avocado, halved and diced
- 1 garlic clove, minced
- 2 peaches, seeded and diced
- Juice of 1 lime
- Salt to taste

DIRECTIONS:

1. In a shallow dish, mix all swordfish marinade ingredients except fillet. Mix well then add fillets to marinate. Place in refrigerator for at least an hour.
2. Meanwhile, create salsa by mixing all salsa ingredients in a medium bowl. Put in the refrigerator to cool.
3. Preheat grill and grill fish on medium fire after marinating until cooked around 4 minutes per side.
4. Place each cooked fillet on a serving plate, top with half of the salsa, serve and enjoy.

NUTRITION: Calories: 416 Carbs: 21g Protein: 30g Fat: 23.5g

Breaded and Spiced Halibut

Preparation time: 10 minutes.
Level: Easy.
Cooking time: 15 minutes.
Servings: 4
INGREDIENTS:

- ¼ cup chopped fresh chives
- ¼ cup chopped fresh dill
- ¼ teaspoon ground black pepper
- ¾ cup panko breadcrumbs
- 1 tablespoon extra-virgin olive oil
- 1 teaspoon finely grated lemon zest
- 1 teaspoon sea salt
- 1/3 cup chopped fresh parsley
- 4 pieces of 6 ounces halibut fillets

DIRECTIONS:

1. Line a baking sheet with foil, grease with cooking spray, and preheat the oven to 400°F.
2. In a small bowl, mix black pepper, sea salt, lemon zest, olive oil, chives, dill, parsley, and breadcrumbs. If needed, add more salt to taste. Set aside.
3. Meanwhile, wash halibut fillets on cold tap water. Dry with paper towels and place on prepared baking sheet.
4. Generously spoon crumb mixture onto halibut fillets. Ensure that fillets are covered with crumb mixture. Press down on crumb mixture onto each fillet.
5. Pop into the oven and bake for 10–15 minutes or until fish is flaky and the crumb topping is already lightly browned.

NUTRITION: Calories: 336.4 Protein: 25.3g Fat: 25.3g Carbs: 4.1g

Berries and Grilled Calamari

Preparation time: 10 minutes.
Level: Easy.
Cooking time: 5 minutes.
Servings: 4
INGREDIENTS:

- ¼ cup dried cranberries
- ¼ cup extra-virgin olive oil
- ¼ cup olive oil
- ¼ cup sliced almonds
- ½ lemon, juiced
- ¾ cup blueberries
- 1(½) pounds calamari tube, cleaned
- 1 granny smith apple, sliced thinly
- 1 tablespoon fresh lemon juice
- 2 tablespoons apple cider vinegar
- 6 cups fresh spinach
- Freshly grated pepper to taste
- Sea salt to taste

DIRECTIONS:
1. In a small bowl, make the vinaigrette by mixing well the tablespoon of lemon juice, apple cider vinegar, and extra-virgin olive oil. Season with pepper and salt to taste. Set aside.
2. Turn on the grill to medium fire and let the grates heat up for a minute or two.
3. In a large bowl, add olive oil and the calamari tube. Season calamari generously with pepper and salt.
4. Place seasoned and oiled calamari onto heated grate and grill until cooked or opaque. This is around two minutes per side.
5. As you wait for the calamari to cook, you can combine almonds, cranberries, blueberries, spinach, and the thinly sliced apple in a large salad bowl. Toss to mix.
6. Remove cooked calamari from the grill and transfer it on a chopping board. Cut into ¼-inch thick rings and throw them into the salad bowl.
7. Drizzle with vinaigrette and toss well to coat the salad.
8. Serve and enjoy!

NUTRITION: Calories: 567 Fat: 24.5g Protein: 54.8g Carbs: 30.6g

Coconut Salsa on Chipotle Fish Tacos

Preparation time: 10 minutes.
Level: Easy.
Cooking time: 10 minutes.
Servings: 4
INGREDIENTS:

- ¼ cup chopped fresh cilantro
- ½ cup seeded and finely chopped plum tomato
- 1 cup peeled and finely chopped mango
- 1 lime cut into wedges
- 1 tablespoon chipotle Chile powder
- 1 tablespoon safflower oil
- 1/3 cup finely chopped red onion
- 10 tablespoons fresh lime juice, divided
- 4(6-ounces) boneless, skinless cod fillets
- 5 tablespoons dried unsweetened shredded coconut
- 8 pieces of 6-inch tortillas, heated

DIRECTIONS:

1. Whisk well Chile powder, oil, and 4 tablespoons of lime juice in a glass baking dish. Add cod and marinate for 12–15 minutes. Turning once halfway through the marinating time.
2. Make the salsa by mixing coconut, 6 tablespoons of lime juice, cilantro, onions, tomatoes, and mangoes in a medium bowl. Set aside.
3. On high, heat a grill pan. Place cod and grill for four minutes per side turning only once.
4. Once cooked, slice cod into large flakes and evenly divide onto tortilla.
5. Evenly divide salsa on top of cod and serve with a side of lime wedges.

NUTRITION: Calories: 477 Protein: 35.0g Fat: 12.4g Carbs: 57.4g

Baked Cod Crusted with Herbs

Preparation time: 5 minutes.
Level: Easy.
Cooking time: 10 minutes.
Servings: 4
INGREDIENTS:

- ¼ cup honey
- ¼ teaspoon salt
- ½ cup panko
- ½ teaspoon pepper
- 1 tablespoon extra-virgin olive oil
- 1 tablespoon lemon juice
- 1 teaspoon dried basil
- 1 teaspoon dried parsley
- 1 teaspoon rosemary
- 4 pieces of 4 ounces cod fillets

DIRECTIONS:

1. With olive oil, grease a 9 x 13-inch baking pan and preheat the oven to 375°F.
2. In a zip-top bag mix panko, rosemary, salt, pepper, parsley, and basil.
3. Evenly spread cod fillets in prepped dish and drizzle with lemon juice.
4. Then brush the fillets with honey on all sides. Discard the remaining honey, if any.
5. Then evenly divide the panko mixture on top of cod fillets.
6. Pop in the oven and bake for ten minutes or until fish is cooked.
7. Serve and enjoy.

NUTRITION: Calories: 137 Protein: 5g Fat: 2g Carbs: 21g

Creamy Bacon-Fish Chowder

Preparation time: 10 minutes.
Level: Average.
Cooking time: 30 minutes.
Servings: 4
INGREDIENTS:

- 1(1/2) pounds cod
- 1(1/2) teaspoon dried thyme
- 1 large onion, chopped
- 1 medium carrot, coarsely chopped
- 1 tablespoon butter, cut into small pieces
- 1 teaspoon salt, divided
- 3(1/2) cups baking potato, peeled and cubed
- 3 slices uncooked bacon
- 3/4 teaspoons freshly ground black pepper, divided
- 4(1/2) cups water
- 4 bay leaves
- 4 cups 2% reduced-fat milk

DIRECTIONS:

1. In a large skillet, add the water and bay leaves and let it simmer. Add the fish. Cover and let it simmer some more until the flesh flakes easily with a fork. Remove the fish from the skillet and cut it into large pieces. Set aside the cooking liquid.
2. Place Dutch oven on medium heat and cook the bacon until crisp. Remove the bacon and reserve the bacon drippings. Crush the bacon and set it aside.
3. Stir potato, onion, and carrot in the pan with the bacon drippings, cook over medium heat for 10 minutes. Add the cooking liquid, bay leaves, 1/2 teaspoon of salt, 1/4 teaspoon of pepper, and thyme, let it boil. Lower the heat and let simmer for 10 minutes. Add the milk and butter, simmer until the potatoes become tender, but do not boil. Add the fish, 1/2 teaspoon of salt, 1/2 teaspoon of pepper. Remove the bay leaves.
4. Serve sprinkled with the crushed bacon.

NUTRITION: Calories: 400 Carbs: 34.5g Protein: 20.8g Fat: 19.7g

Trout and Peppers Mix

Preparation time: 10 minutes.
Level: Average.
Cooking time: 20 minutes.
Servings: 4
INGREDIENTS:

- 4 trout fillets, boneless
- 2 tablespoons kalamata olives, pitted and chopped
- 1 tablespoon capers, drained
- 2 tablespoons olive oil
- A pinch of salt and black pepper
- 1(½) teaspoon chili powder
- 1 yellow bell pepper, chopped
- 1 red bell pepper, chopped
- 1 green bell pepper, chopped

DIRECTIONS:

1. Heat up a pan with the oil over medium-high heat, add the trout, salt, and pepper and cook for 10 minutes.
2. Flip the fish, add the peppers and the rest of the ingredients, cook for 10 minutes more, divide the whole mix between plates and serve.

NUTRITION: Calories: 572 Fat: 17.4g Fiber: 6g Carbs: 71g Protein: 33.7g

Crisped Coco-Shrimp with Mango Dip

Preparation time: 10 minutes.
Level: Average.
Cooking time: 20 minutes.
Servings: 4
INGREDIENTS:

- 1 cup shredded coconut
- 1 pound raw shrimp, peeled and deveined
- 2 egg whites
- 4 tablespoons tapioca starch
- Pepper and salt to taste

Mango dip ingredients:

- 1 cup mango, chopped
- 1 jalapeno, thinly minced
- 1 teaspoon lime juice
- 1/3 cup coconut milk
- 3 teaspoons raw honey

DIRECTIONS:

1. Preheat the oven to 400°F.
2. Ready a pan with a wire rack on top.
3. In a medium bowl, add tapioca starch, and season with pepper and salt.
4. In a second medium bowl, add egg whites and whisk.
5. In a third medium bowl, add coconut.
6. To ready shrimps, dip first in tapioca starch, then egg whites, and then coconut. Place dredged shrimp on a wire rack. Repeat until all shrimps are covered.
7. Pop shrimp in the oven and roast for 10 minutes per side.
8. Meanwhile, make the dip by adding all the ingredients to a blender. Puree until smooth and creamy. Transfer to a dipping bowl.
9. Once shrimps are golden brown, serve with mango dip.

NUTRITION: Calories: 294.2 Protein: 26.6g Fat: 7g Carbs: 31.2g

Cucumber-Basil Salsa on Halibut Pouches

Preparation time: 10 minutes.
Level: Easy.
Cooking time: 17 minutes.
Servings: 4
INGREDIENTS:

- 1 lime, thinly sliced into 8 pieces
- 2 cups mustard greens, stems removed
- 2 teaspoons olive oil
- 4–5 radishes trimmed and quartered
- 4(4-ounces skinless halibut filets
- 4 large fresh basil leaves
- Cayenne pepper to taste, optional
- Pepper and salt to taste

Salsa ingredients:

- 1(½) cups diced cucumber
- 1(½) finely chopped fresh basil leaves
- 2 teaspoons fresh lime juice
- Pepper and salt to taste

DIRECTIONS:

1. Preheat the oven to 400°F.
2. Prepare parchment papers by making 4 pieces of 15 x 12-inch rectangles. Lengthwise, fold in half and unfold pieces on the table.
3. Season halibut fillets with pepper, salt, and cayenne—if using cayenne.
4. Just to the right of the fold going lengthwise, place ½ cup of mustard greens. Add a basil leaf to the center of mustard greens and topped with 1 lime slice. Around the greens, layer ¼ of the radishes. Drizzle with ½ teaspoon of oil, season with pepper and salt. Top it with a slice of halibut fillet.
5. Just as you would make a calzone, fold the parchment paper over your filling and crimp the edges of the parchment paper beginning from one end to the other end. To seal the end of the crimped parchment paper, pinch it.
6. Repeat the process with the remaining ingredients until you have 4 pieces of parchment paper filled with halibut and greens.
7. Place pouches in a baking pan and bake in the oven until halibut is flaky around 15 to 17 minutes.
8. While waiting for halibut pouches to cook, make your salsa by mixing all the salsa ingredients in a medium bowl.
9. Once halibut is cooked, remove it from the oven and make a tear on top. Be careful of the steam as it is very hot. Equally, divide salsa and spoon ¼ of salsa on top of halibut through the slit you have created.

NUTRITION: Calories: 335.4 Protein: 20.2g Fat: 16.3g Carbs: 22.1g

Dijon Mustard and Lime Marinated Shrimp

Preparation time: 10 minutes.
Level: Easy.
Cooking time: 10 minutes.
Servings: 4

INGREDIENTS:

- ½ cup fresh lime juice, plus lime zest as garnish
- ½ cup rice vinegar
- ½ teaspoons hot sauce
- 1 bay leaf
- 1 cup water
- 1 pound uncooked shrimp, peeled and deveined
- 1 medium red onion, chopped
- 2 tablespoons capers
- 2 tablespoons Dijon mustard
- 3 whole cloves

DIRECTIONS:

1. Mix hot sauce, mustard, capers, lime juice, and onion in a shallow baking dish and set aside.
2. Bring to a boil in a large saucepan bay leaf, cloves, vinegar, and water.
3. Once boiling, add shrimps and cook for a minute while stirring continuously.
4. Drain shrimps and pour shrimps into the onion mixture.
5. For an hour, refrigerate while covered the shrimps.
6. Then serve shrimps cold and garnished with lime zest.

NUTRITION: Calories: 232.2 Protein: 17.8g Fat: 3g Carbs: 15g

Dill Relish on White Sea Bass

Preparation time: 10 minutes.
Level: Easy.
Cooking time: 12 minutes.
Servings: 4
INGREDIENTS:
- 1(½) tablespoon chopped white onion
- 1(½) teaspoon chopped fresh dill
- 1 lemon, quartered
- 1 teaspoon Dijon mustard
- 1 teaspoon lemon juice
- 1 teaspoon pickled baby capers, drained
- 4 pieces of 4 ounces white sea bass fillets

DIRECTIONS:
1. Preheat the oven to 375°F.
2. Mix lemon juice, mustard, dill, capers, and onions in a small bowl.
3. Prepare four aluminum foil squares and place 1 fillet per foil.
4. Squeeze a lemon wedge per fish.
5. Evenly divide into 4 the dill spread and drizzle over the fillet.
6. Close the foil over the fish securely and pop it in the oven.
7. Bake for 10 to 12 minutes or until fish is cooked through.
8. Remove from foil and transfer to a serving platter, serve and enjoy.

NUTRITION: Calories: 115 Protein: 7g Fat: 1g Carbs: 12g

Garlic Roasted Shrimp with Zucchini Pasta

Preparation time: 10 minutes.
Level: Easy.
Cooking time: 10 minutes.
Servings: 4
INGREDIENTS:

- 2 medium-sized zucchinis, cut into thin strips or spaghetti noodles
- Salt and pepper to taste
- 1 lemon, peeled and juiced
- 2 garlic cloves, minced
- 2 tablespoons ghee, melted
- 2 tablespoons olive oil
- 8 ounces shrimps, cleaned and deveined

DIRECTIONS:

1. Preheat the oven to 400°F.
2. In a mixing bowl, mix all the ingredients except the zucchini noodles. Toss to coat the shrimp.
3. Bake for 10 minutes until the shrimps turn pink.
4. Add the zucchini pasta then toss.

NUTRITION: Calories: 299 Fat: 23.2g Protein: 14.3g Carbs: 10.9g

Easy Seafood French Stew

Preparation time: 10 minutes.
Level: Difficult.
Cooking time: 45 minutes.
Servings: 4
INGREDIENTS:

- Pepper and salt to taste
- ½ pound littleneck clams
- ½ pound mussels
- 1 pound shrimp, peeled and deveined
- 1 large lobster
- 2 pound assorted small whole fresh fish, scaled and cleaned
- 2 tablespoons parsley, finely chopped
- 2 tablespoons garlic, chopped
- 1 cup fennel, julienned
- Juice and zest of one orange
- 3 cups tomatoes, peeled, seeded, and chopped
- 1 cup leeks, julienned
- Pinch of Saffron

Stew ingredients:

- 1 cup white wine
- 2 cups Water
- 1 pound fish bones
- 2 sprigs thyme
- 8 peppercorns
- 1 bay leaf
- 3 cloves garlic
- Salt and pepper
- 1/2 cup chopped celery
- 1/2 cup chopped onion
- 2 tablespoons olive oil

DIRECTIONS:

1. Do the stew: Heat oil in a large saucepan. Sauté the celery and onions for 3 minutes. Season with pepper and salt. Stir in the garlic and cook for about a minute. Add the thyme, peppercorns, and bay leaves. Stir in the wine, water, and fish bones. Let it boil then before reducing to a simmer. Take the pan off the fire and strain the broth into another container.
2. For the Bouillabaisse: Bring the strained broth to a simmer and stir in the parsley, leeks, orange juice, orange zest, garlic, fennel, tomatoes, and saffron. Sprinkle with pepper and salt. Stir in the lobsters and fish. Let it simmer for eight minutes before stirring in the clams, mussels, and shrimps. For six minutes, allow cooking while covered before seasoning again with pepper and salt. Assemble in a shallow dish all the seafood and pour the broth over it.

NUTRITION: Calories: 348 Carbs: 20.0g Protein: 31.8g Fat: 15.2g

Fresh and No-Cook Oysters

Preparation time: 10 minutes.
Level: Easy.
Cooking time: 5 minutes.
Servings: 4
INGREDIENTS:

- 2 lemons
- 24 medium oysters
- Tabasco sauce for serving

DIRECTIONS:

1. If you are a newbie when it comes to eating oysters, then I suggest that you blanch the oysters before eating.
2. For some, eating oysters raw is a great way to enjoy this dish because of the consistency and juiciness of raw oysters. Plus, adding lemon juice before eating the raw oysters cooks it a bit.
3. So, to blanch oysters, bring a big pot of water to a rolling boil. Add oysters in batches of 6–10 pieces. Leave on a boiling pot of water between 3–5 minutes and remove oysters right away. To eat oysters, squeeze lemon juice on the oyster on the shell, add tabasco as desired, and eat.

NUTRITION: Calories: 247 Protein: 29g Fat: 7g Carbs: 17g

Easy Broiled Lobster Tails

Preparation time: 10 minutes.
Level: Easy.
Cooking time: 10 minutes.
Servings: 4
INGREDIENTS:

- 1(6-ounces) frozen lobster tails
- 1 tablespoon olive oil
- 1 teaspoon lemon-pepper seasoning

DIRECTIONS:

1. Preheat the oven broiler.
2. With kitchen scissors, cut thawed lobster tails in half lengthwise.
3. Brush with oil the exposed lobster meat. Season with lemon-pepper.
4. Place lobster tails on a baking sheet with exposed meat facing up.
5. Place on top broiler rack and broil for 10 minutes until lobster meat is lightly browned on the sides and center meat is opaque. Serve and enjoy.

NUTRITION: Calories: 175.6 Protein: 23g Fat: 10g Carbs: 18.4g

Ginger Scallion Sauce over Seared Ahi

Preparation time: 10 minutes.
Level: Easy.
Cooking time: 6 minutes.
Servings: 4
INGREDIENTS:

- 1 bunch scallions, bottoms removed, finely chopped
- 1 tablespoon rice wine vinegar
- 16 ounces Ahi tuna steaks
- 2 tablespoons fresh ginger, peeled and grated
- 3 tablespoons coconut oil, melted
- Pepper and salt to taste
- ½ cup Soy sauce

DIRECTIONS:

1. In a small bowl mix together vinegar, 2 tablespoons of oil, soy sauce, ginger, and scallions. Put aside.
2. On medium fire, place a large saucepan and heat the remaining oil. Once the oil is hot and starts to smoke, sear tuna until deeply browned or for two minutes per side.
3. Place seared tuna on a serving platter and let it stand for 5 minutes before slicing into 1-inch-thick strips.
4. Drizzle ginger-scallion mixture over seared tuna, serve, and enjoy.

NUTRITION: Calories: 247 Protein: 29g Fat: 1g Carbs: 8g

Healthy Poached Trout

Preparation time: 10 minutes.
Level: Easy.
Cooking time: 10 minutes.
Servings: 4
INGREDIENTS:

- 1(8-ounces) boneless, skin-on trout fillet
- 2 cups chicken broth or water
- 2 leeks, halved
- 6-8 slices lemon
- Salt and pepper to taste

DIRECTIONS:

1. On medium fire, place a large nonstick skillet and arrange leeks and lemons on a pan in a layer. Cover with soup stock or water and bring to a simmer.
2. Meanwhile, season trout on both sides with pepper and salt. Place trout on a simmering pan of water. Cover and cook until trout is flaky, around 8 minutes.
3. In a serving platter, spoon leek and lemons on the bottom of a plate, top with trout, and spoon sauce into a plate. Serve and enjoy.

NUTRITION: Calories: 360.2 Protein: 13.8g Fat: 7.5g Carbs: 51.5g

Leftover Salmon Salad Power Bowls

Preparation time: 10 minutes.
Level: Easy.
Cooking time: 10 minutes.
Servings: 4
INGREDIENTS:

- ½ cup raspberries
- ½ cup zucchini, sliced
- 1 lemon, juice squeezed
- 1 tablespoon balsamic glaze
- 2 sprigs of thyme, chopped
- 2 tablespoons olive oil
- 4 cups seasonal greens
- 4 ounces leftover grilled salmon
- Salt and pepper to taste

DIRECTIONS:

1. Heat oil in a skillet over medium flame and sauté the zucchini. Season with salt and pepper to taste.
2. In a mixing bowl, mix all the ingredients together.
3. Toss to combine everything.
4. Sprinkle with nut cheese.

NUTRITION: Calories: 450.3 Fat: 35.5g Protein: 23.4g Carbs: 9.3g

Lemon-Garlic Baked Halibut

Preparation time: 10 minutes.
Level: Easy.
Cooking time: 15 minutes.
Servings: 4
INGREDIENTS:

- 1 large garlic clove, minced
- 1 tablespoon chopped flat-leaf parsley
- 1 teaspoon olive oil
- 2(5-ounces) boneless, skin-on halibut fillets
- 2 teaspoons lemon zest
- Juice of ½ lemon, divided
- Salt and pepper to taste

DIRECTIONS:

1. Grease a baking dish with cooking spray and preheat the oven to 400°F.
2. Place halibut with skin touching the dish and drizzle with olive oil.
3. Season with pepper and salt.
4. Pop into the oven and bake until flaky around 12–15 minutes.
5. Remove from the oven and drizzle with the remaining lemon juice, serve and enjoy with a side of salad greens.

NUTRITION: Calories: 315.3 Protein: 14.1g Fat: 10.5g Carbs: 36.6g

Minty-Cucumber Yogurt Topped Grilled Fish

Preparation time: 10 minutes.
Level: Easy.
Cooking time: 2 minutes.
Servings: 4
INGREDIENTS:

- ¼ cup 2% plain Greek yogurt
- ¼ teaspoon + 1/8 teaspoon salt
- ¼ teaspoon black pepper
- ½ green onion, finely chopped
- ½ teaspoon dried oregano
- 1 tablespoon finely chopped fresh mint leaves
- 3 tablespoons finely chopped English cucumber
- 4(5-ounces) cod fillets
- Cooking oil as needed

DIRECTIONS:

1. Brush grill grate with oil and preheat grill to high.
2. Season cod fillets on both sides with pepper, ¼ teaspoon of salt, and oregano.
3. Grill cod for 3 minutes per side or until cooked to desired doneness.
4. Mix thoroughly 1/8 teaspoon of salt, onion, mint, cucumber, and yogurt in a small bowl. Serve cod with a dollop of the dressing. This dish can be paired with salad greens or brown rice.

NUTRITION: Calories: 253.5 Protein: 25.5g Fat: 1g Carbs: 5g

One-Pot Seafood Chowder

Preparation time: 10 minutes.
Level: Easy.
Cooking time: 10 minutes.
Servings: 3
INGREDIENTS:

- 3 cans coconut milk
- 1 tablespoon garlic, minced
- Salt and pepper to taste
- 3 cans clams, chopped
- 2 cans shrimps, canned
- 1 package fresh shrimps, shelled and deveined
- 1 can corn, drained
- 4 large potatoes, diced
- 2 carrots, peeled and chopped
- 2 celery stalks, chopped

DIRECTIONS:

1. Place all the ingredients in a pot and give a good stir to mix everything.
2. Close the lid and turn on the heat to medium.
3. Bring to a boil and allow simmering for 10 minutes.
4. Place in individual containers.
5. Put a label and store it in the fridge.
6. Allow warming at room temperature before heating in the microwave oven.

NUTRITION: Calories: 532 Carbs: 92.5g Protein: 25.3g Fat: 6.7g

Orange Rosemary Seared Salmon

Preparation time: 10 minutes.
Level: Easy.
Cooking time: 10 minutes.
Servings: 4
INGREDIENTS:

- ½ cup chicken stock
- 1 cup fresh orange juice
- 1 tablespoon coconut oil
- 1 tablespoon tapioca starch
- 2 garlic cloves, minced
- 2 tablespoons fresh lemon juice
- 2 teaspoons fresh rosemary, minced
- 2 teaspoons orange zest
- 4 salmon fillets, skins removed
- Salt and pepper to taste

DIRECTIONS:

1. Season the salmon fillet on both sides.
2. In a skillet, heat coconut oil over medium-high heat. Cook the salmon fillets for 5 minutes on each side. Set aside.
3. In a mixing bowl, combine the orange juice, chicken stock, lemon juice, and orange zest.
4. In the skillet, sauté the garlic and rosemary for 2 minutes and pour the orange juice mixture. Bring to a boil. Lower the heat to medium-low and simmer. Season with salt and pepper to taste.
5. Pour the sauce all over the salmon fillet then serve.

NUTRITION: Calories: 493 Fat: 17.9g Protein: 66.7g Carbs: 12.8g

Orange Herbed Sauced White Bass

Preparation time: 10 minutes.
Level: Average.
Cooking time: 33 minutes.
Servings: 4
INGREDIENTS:

- ¼ cup thinly sliced green onions
- ½ cup orange juice
- 1(½) tablespoon fresh lemon juice
- 1(½) tablespoon olive oil
- 1 large onion, halved, thinly sliced
- 1 large orange, unpeeled, sliced
- 3 tablespoons chopped fresh dill
- 6(3-ounces) skinless white bass fillets
- Additional unpeeled orange slices

DIRECTIONS:

1. Grease a 13 x 9-inch glass baking dish and preheat the oven to 400°F.
2. Arrange orange slices in a single layer on a baking dish, top with onion slices, seasoned with pepper and salt plus drizzled with oil.
3. Pop in the oven and roast for 25 minutes or until onions are tender and browned.
4. Remove from the oven and increased oven temperature to 450°F. Push onion and orange slices on the sides of the dish and place bass fillets in the middle of the dish. Season with 1(½) tablespoon of dill, pepper, and salt. Arrange onions and orange slices on top of fish and pop them into the oven.
5. Roast for 8 minutes or until salmon is opaque and flaky.
6. In a small bowl, mix 1(½) tablespoon of dill, lemon juice, green onions, and orange juice.
7. Transfer salmon to a serving plate, discard roasted onions, drizzle with the newly made orange sauce, and garnish with fresh orange slices. Serve and enjoy.

NUTRITION: Calories: 312.42 Protein: 84.22 Fat: 23.14 Carbs: 33.91g

Pan Fried Tuna with Herbs and Nut

Preparation time: 10 minutes.
Level: Easy.
Cooking time: 5 minutes.
Servings: 4
INGREDIENTS:

- ¼ cup almonds, chopped finely
- ¼ cup fresh tangerine juice
- ½ teaspoon fennel seeds, chopped finely
- ½ teaspoon ground pepper, divided
- ½ teaspoon sea salt, divided
- 1 tablespoon olive oil
- 2 tablespoons fresh mint, chopped finely
- 2 tablespoons red onion, chopped finely
- 4 pieces of 6-ounces Tuna steak cut in half

DIRECTIONS:

1. Mix fennel seeds, olive oil, mint, onion, tangerine juice, and almonds in a small bowl. Season with ¼ each of pepper and salt.
2. Season fish with the remaining pepper and salt.
3. On medium-high fire, place a large nonstick fry pan and grease with cooking spray.
4. Pan-fry tuna until the desired doneness is reached or for one minute per side.
5. Transfer cooked tuna to a serving plate, drizzle with dressing, and serve.

NUTRITION: Calories: 272 Fat: 9.7g Protein: 42g Carbs: 4.2g

Paprika Salmon and Green Beans

Preparation time: 10 minutes.
Level: Average.
Cooking time: 20 minutes.
Servings: 4
INGREDIENTS:

- ¼ cup olive oil
- ½ tablespoon onion powder
- ½ teaspoon cayenne pepper
- 1 tablespoon smoked paprika
- 1 pound green beans
- 2 teaspoons minced garlic
- 3 tablespoons fresh herbs
- 6 ounces of salmon steak
- Salt and pepper to taste

DIRECTIONS:

1. Preheat the oven to 400°F.
2. Grease a baking sheet and set it aside.
3. Heat a skillet over medium-low heat and add the olive oil. Sauté the garlic, smoked paprika, fresh herbs, cayenne pepper, and onion powder. Stir for a minute then let the mixture sit for 5 minutes. Set aside.
4. Put the salmon steaks in a bowl and add salt and the paprika spice mixture. Rub to coat the salmon well.
5. Place the salmon on the baking sheet and cook for 18 minutes.
6. Meanwhile, blanch the green beans in boiling water with salt.
7. Serve the beans with the salmon.

NUTRITION: Calories: 945.8 Fat: 66.6g Protein: 43.5g Carbs: 43.1g

Pesto and Lemon Halibut

Preparation time: 10 minutes.
Level: Easy.
Cooking time: 10 minutes.
Servings: 4
INGREDIENTS:

- 1 tablespoon fresh lemon juice
- 1 tablespoon lemon rind, grated
- 2 garlic cloves, peeled
- 2 tablespoons olive oil
- ¼ cup Parmesan Cheese, freshly grated
- 2/3 cups firmly packed basil leaves
- 1/8 teaspoon freshly ground black pepper
- ¼ teaspoon salt, divided
- 4 pieces 6-ounces halibut fillets

DIRECTIONS:

1. Preheat grill to medium fire and grease grate with cooking spray.
2. Season fillets with pepper and 1/8 teaspoon of salt. Place on grill and cook until halibut is flaky around 4 minutes per side.
3. Meanwhile, make your lemon pesto by combining lemon juice, lemon rind, garlic, olive oil, Parmesan cheese, basil leaves, and the remaining salt in a blender. Pulse mixture until finely minced but not pureed.
4. Once fish is done cooking, transfer to a serving platter, pour over the lemon pesto sauce, serve and enjoy.

NUTRITION: Calories: 277.4 Fat: 13g Protein: 38.7g Carbs: 1.4g

Roasted Halibut with Banana Relish

Preparation time: 10 minutes.
Level: Easy.
Cooking time: 12 minutes.
Servings: 4
INGREDIENTS:

- ¼ cup cilantro
- ½ teaspoon freshly grated orange zest
- ½ teaspoon kosher salt, divided
- 1 pound halibut or any deep-water fish
- 1 teaspoon ground coriander, divided into half
- 2 oranges (peeled, segmented, and chopped)
- 2 ripe bananas, diced
- 2 tablespoons lime juice

DIRECTIONS:

1. In a pan, prepare the fish by rubbing ½ teaspoon of coriander and ¼ teaspoon of kosher salt.
2. Place in a baking sheet with cooking spray and bake for 8 to 12 minutes inside a 450°F preheated oven.
3. Prepare the relish by stirring the orange zest, bananas, chopped oranges, lime juice, cilantro, and the rest of the salt and coriander in a medium bowl.
4. Spoon the relish over the roasted fish.
5. Serve and enjoy.

NUTRITION: Calories: 245.7 Protein: 15.3g Fat: 6g Carbs: 21g

Scallops in Wine 'n Olive Oil

Preparation time: 10 minutes.
Level: Easy.
Cooking time: 8 minutes.
Servings: 4
INGREDIENTS:

- ¼ teaspoon salt
- ½ cup dry white wine
- 1(½) pound large sea scallops
- 1(½) teaspoon chopped fresh tarragon
- 2 tablespoons olive oil
- Black pepper, optional

DIRECTIONS:

1. On medium-high fire, place a large nonstick fry pan and heat oil.
2. Add scallops and fry for 3 minutes per side or until edges are lightly browned. Transfer to a serving plate.
3. On the same pan, add salt, tarragon, and wine while scraping the pan to loosen browned bits. Turn off the fire.
4. Pour sauce over scallops and serve.

NUTRITION: Calories: 205.2 Fat: 8g Protein: 28.6g Carbs: 4.7g

Seafood Stew Cioppino

Preparation time: 10 minutes.
Level: Difficult.
Cooking time: 40 minutes.
Servings: 4
INGREDIENTS:

- ¼ cup Italian parsley, chopped
- ¼ teaspoon dried basil
- ¼ teaspoon dried thyme
- ½ cup dry white wine like pinot grigio
- ½ pounds King crab legs, cut at each joint
- ½ onion, chopped
- ½ teaspoon red pepper flakes (adjust to the desired spiciness)
- 1(28-ounces) can crush tomatoes
- 1 pound Mahi midsolo, cut into ½-inch cubes
- 1 pound raw shrimp
- 1 tablespoon olive oil
- 2 bay leaves
- 2 cups clam juice
- 50 live clams, washed
- 6 cloves garlic, minced
- Pepper and salt to taste

DIRECTIONS:

1. On medium fire, place a stockpot and heat oil.
2. Add onion and for 4 minutes sauté until soft.
3. Add bay leaves, thyme, basil, red pepper flakes, and garlic. Cook for a minute while stirring a bit.
4. Add clam juice and tomatoes. Once simmering, place fire to medium-low and cook for 20 minutes uncovered.
5. Add white wine and clams. Cover and cook for 5 minutes or until clams have slightly opened.
6. Stir pot, then add fish pieces, crab legs, and shrimps. Do not stir the soup to maintain the fish's shape. Cook covered for 4 minutes or until the clams open and the fish and shrimps are opaque and cooked.
7. Season with pepper and salt to taste.
8. Transfer Cioppino to serving bowls and garnish with parsley before serving.

NUTRITION: Calories: 371 Carbs: 15.5g Protein: 62g Fat: 6.8g

Simple Cod Piccata

Preparation time: 10 minutes.
Level: Easy.
Cooking time: 15 minutes.
Servings: 4
INGREDIENTS:

- ¼ cup capers, drained
- ½ teaspoon salt
- ¾ cup chicken stock
- 1/3 cup almond flour
- 1 pound cod fillets, patted dry
- 2 tablespoons fresh parsley, chopped
- 2 tablespoons grapeseed oil
- 3 tablespoons extra-virgin oil
- 3 tablespoons lemon juice

DIRECTIONS:

1. In a bowl, combine the almond flour and salt.
2. Dredge the fish in the almond flour to coat. Set aside.
3. Heat a little bit of olive oil to coat a large skillet. Heat the skillet over medium-high heat. Add grapeseed oil. Cook the cod for 3 minutes on each side to brown. Remove from the plate and place on a paper towel-lined plate.
4. In a saucepan, mix together the chicken stock, capers, and lemon juice. Simmer to reduce the sauce to half. Add the remaining grapeseed oil.
5. Drizzle the fried cod with the sauce and sprinkle with parsley.

NUTRITION: Calories: 277.1 Fat: 28.3g Protein: 21.9g Carbs: 3.7g

Smoked Trout Tartine

Preparation time: 10 minutes.
Level: Easy.
Cooking time: 0 minutes.
Servings: 4
INGREDIENTS:

- ½ (15-ounces) can cannellini beans
- ½ cup diced roasted red peppers
- ¾ pounds smoked trout, flaked into bite-sized pieces
- 1 stalk celery, finely chopped
- 1 tablespoon extra-virgin olive oil
- 1 teaspoon chopped fresh dill
- 1 teaspoon Dijon mustard
- 2 tablespoons capers, rinsed and drained
- 2 tablespoons freshly squeezed lemon juice
- 2 teaspoons minced onion
- 4 large whole-grain bread, toasted
- Dill sprigs, for garnish
- Pinch of sugar

DIRECTIONS:

1. Mix sugar, mustard, olive oil, and lemon juice in a big bowl.
2. Add the rest of the ingredients except for toasted bread.
3. Toss to mix well.
4. Evenly divide fish mixture on top of bread slices and garnish with dill sprigs.
5. Serve and enjoy.

NUTRITION: Calories: 348.1 Protein: 28.2g Fat: 10.1g Carbs: 36.1g

Tasty Tuna Scaloppine

Preparation time: 10 minutes.
Level: Easy.
Cooking time: 10 minutes.
Servings: 4
INGREDIENTS:

- ¼ cup chopped almonds
- ¼ cup fresh tangerine juice
- ½ teaspoon fennel seeds
- ½ teaspoon ground black pepper, divided
- ½ teaspoon salt
- 1 tablespoon extra-virgin olive oil
- 2 tablespoons chopped fresh mint
- 2 tablespoons chopped red onion
- 4(6-ounces) sushi-grade Yellowfin tuna steaks, each split in half horizontally
- Cooking spray

DIRECTIONS:

1. In a small bowl mix fennel seeds, olive oil, mint, onion, tangerine juice, almonds, ¼ teaspoon of pepper, and ¼ teaspoon of salt. Combine thoroughly.
2. Season fish with the remaining salt and pepper.
3. On medium-high fire, place a large nonstick pan and grease with cooking spray. Pan-fry fish in two batches, cooking each side for a minute.
4. Fish is best served with a side of salad greens or a half cup of cooked brown rice.

NUTRITION: Calories: 405 Protein: 27.5g Fat: 11.9g Carbs: 27.5

Thyme and Lemon on Baked Salmon

Preparation time: 10 minutes.
Level: Average.
Cooking time: 25 minutes.
Servings: 4
INGREDIENTS:

- 1(32-ounces) salmon fillet
- 1 lemon, sliced thinly
- 1 tablespoon capers
- 1 tablespoon fresh thyme
- Olive oil for drizzling
- Pepper and salt to taste

DIRECTIONS:

1. In a foil-lined baking sheet, place a parchment paper on top.
2. Place salmon with skin side down on parchment paper.
3. Season generously with pepper and salt.
4. Place capers on top of the fillet. Cover with thinly sliced lemon. Garnish with thyme.
5. Pop in a cold oven and bake for 25 minutes at 400°F settings.
6. Serve right away and enjoy.

NUTRITION: Calories: 684.4 Protein: 94.3g Fat: 32.7g Carbs: 4.3g

Chapter 9:
MEAT DISHES

Saffron Chicken Thighs and Green Beans

Preparation time: 10 minutes.
Level: Average.
Cooking time: 25 minutes.
Servings: 4
INGREDIENTS:
- 2 pounds chicken thighs, boneless and skinless
- 2 teaspoons saffron powder
- 1-pound green beans, trimmed and halved
- ½ cup Greek yogurt
- Salt and black pepper to taste
- 1 tablespoon lime juice
- 1 tablespoon dill, chopped

DIRECTIONS:
1. In a roasting pan, combine the chicken with the saffron, green beans, and the rest of the ingredients, toss a bit, introduce in the oven, and bake at 400°F for 25 minutes.
2. Divide everything between plates and serve.

NUTRITION: Calories: 274 Fat: 12.3g Fiber: 5.3g Carbs: 20.4g Protein: 14.3g

Bold Chorizo Paella

Preparation time: 5 minutes.
Level: Average.
Cooking time: 30 minutes.
Servings: 4
INGREDIENTS:

- 3 tablespoons extra-virgin olive oil
- 1 large onion, chopped
- 2 cloves garlic, minced
- 2 tablespoons tomato paste
- 1 teaspoon paprika
- 1 teaspoon saffron thread
- 1-pound Spanish chorizo sausage
- 2 cups Bomba or Arborio rice
- 1(½) teaspoons salt
- 5 cups water

DIRECTIONS:

1. In a large, deep skillet over medium heat, cook the olive oil and onion for 3 to 5 minutes. Add garlic and cook for another minute.
2. Stir in the tomato paste, paprika, and saffron. Stir in the chorizo and rice, and cook for 3 minutes.
3. Add the salt and water. Stir to combine, turn heat to low, and let simmer for 10 minutes. Give the rice a gentle stir and cook for another 12 to 15 minutes.
4. Serve warm.

NUTRITION: Calories: 747 Protein: 23g Total carbohydrates: 76g Sugars: 2g Fiber: 2g Total fat: 39g Saturated fat: 12g Cholesterol: 80mg Sodium: 1,593mg

Moist Shredded Beef

Preparation time: 10 minutes.
Level: Average.
Cooking time: 20 minutes.
Servings: 4
INGREDIENTS:

- 2 pounds beef chuck roast, cut into chunks
- 1/2 tablespoon dried red pepper
- 1 tablespoon Italian seasoning
- 1 tablespoon garlic, minced
- 2 tablespoons vinegar
- 14 ounces can fire-roasted tomatoes
- 1/2 cup bell pepper, chopped
- 1/2 cup carrots, chopped
- 1 cup onion, chopped
- 1 teaspoon salt

DIRECTIONS:

1. Add all the ingredients into the inner pot of the instant pot and set the pot on sauté mode.
2. Seal pot with the lid and cook on high for 20 minutes.
3. Once done, release pressure using quick release. Remove the lid.
4. Shred the meat using a fork.
5. Stir well and serve.

NUTRITION: Calories: 456 Fat: 32.7g Carbohydrates: 7.7g Sugar: 4.1g Protein: 31g Cholesterol: 118mg

Hearty Beef Ragu

Preparation time: 10 minutes.
Level: Difficult.
Cooking time: 50 minutes.
Servings: 4
INGREDIENTS:

- 1(½) pound beef steak, diced
- 1 1/2 cup beef stock
- 1 tablespoon coconut amino
- 14 ounces can tomato, chopped
- 1/2 teaspoon ground cinnamon
- 1 teaspoon dried oregano
- 1 teaspoon dried thyme
- 1 teaspoon dried basil
- 1 teaspoon paprika
- 1 bay leaf
- 1 tablespoon garlic, chopped
- 1/2 teaspoon cayenne pepper
- 1 celery stick, diced
- 1 carrot, diced
- 1 onion, diced
- 2 tablespoons olive oil
- 1/4 teaspoon pepper
- 1(1/2) teaspoon sea salt

DIRECTIONS:

1. Add oil into the instant pot and set the pot on sauté mode.
2. Add celery, carrots, onion, and salt and sauté for 5 minutes.
3. Add meat and the remaining ingredients and stir everything well.
4. Seal pot with the lid and cook on high for 30 minutes.
5. Once done, allow releasing pressure naturally for 10 minutes then release the rest using the quick release. Remove the lid.
6. Shred meat using a fork. Set pot on sauté mode and cook for 10 minutes. Stir every 2–3 minutes.
7. Serve and enjoy.

NUTRITION: Calories: 435 Fat: 18.1g Carbohydrates: 12.3g Sugar: 5.5g Protein: 54.4g Cholesterol: 152mg

Dill Beef Brisket

Preparation time: 10 minutes.
Level: Difficult.
Cooking time: 50 minutes.
Serving: 4
INGREDIENTS:

- 2(1/2) pounds beef brisket, cut into cubes
- 2(1/2) cups beef stock
- 2 tablespoons dill, chopped
- 1 celery stalk, chopped
- 1 onion, sliced
- 1 tablespoon garlic, minced
- Pepper to taste
- Salt to taste

DIRECTIONS:

1. Add all the ingredients into the inner pot of the instant pot and stir well.
2. Seal pot with the lid and cook on high for 50 minutes.
3. Once done, allow releasing pressure naturally for 10 minutes then release the rest using the quick release. Remove the lid. Serve and enjoy.

NUTRITION: Calories: 556 Fat: 18.1g Carbohydrates: 4.3g Sugar: 1.3g Protein: 88.5g Cholesterol: 253mg

Tasty Beef Stew

Preparation time: 10 minutes.
Level: Average.
Cooking time: 30 minutes.
Serving: 4
INGREDIENTS:

- 2(1/2) pounds beef roast, cut into chunks
- 1 cup beef broth
- 1/2 cup balsamic vinegar
- 1 tablespoon honey
- 1/2 teaspoon red pepper flakes
- 1 tablespoon garlic, minced
- Pepper to taste
- Salt to taste

DIRECTIONS:

1. Add all the ingredients into the inner pot of the instant pot and stir well.
2. Seal pot with the lid and cook on high for 30 minutes.
3. Once done, allow releasing pressure naturally. Remove the lid.
4. Stir well and serve.

NUTRITION: Calories: 562 Fat: 18.1g Carbohydrates: 5.7g Sugar: 4.6g Protein: 87.4g Cholesterol: 253mg

Meatloaf

Preparation time: 10 minutes.
Level: Difficult.
Cooking time: 35 minutes.
Serving: 4
INGREDIENTS:

- 2 pounds ground beef
- 2 eggs, lightly beaten
- 1/4 teaspoon dried basil
- 3 tablespoons olive oil
- 1/2 teaspoon dried sage
- 1(1/2) teaspoon dried parsley
- 1 teaspoon oregano
- 2 teaspoons thyme
- 1 teaspoon rosemary
- Pepper to taste
- Salt to taste

DIRECTIONS:

1. Pour 1(1/2) cups of water into the instant pot then place the trivet in the pot.
2. Spray loaf pan with cooking spray.
3. Add all the ingredients into the mixing bowl and mix until well combined.
4. Transfer the meat mixture into the prepared loaf pan and place the loaf pan on top of the trivet in the pot.
5. Seal pot with the lid and cook on high for 35 minutes.
6. Once done, allow releasing pressure naturally for 10 minutes then release the rest using the quick release. Remove the lid.
7. Serve and enjoy.

NUTRITION: Calories: 365 Fat: 18g Carbohydrates: 0.7g Sugar: 0.1g Protein: 47.8g Cholesterol: 190mg

Flavorful Beef Bourguignon

Preparation time: 10 minutes.
Level: Average.
Cooking time: 20 minutes.
Serving: 4
INGREDIENTS:

- 1(1/2) pound beef chuck roast, cut into chunks
- 2/3 cup beef stock
- 2 tablespoons fresh thyme
- 1 bay leaf
- 1 teaspoon garlic, minced
- 8 ounces mushrooms, sliced
- 2 tablespoons tomato paste
- 2/3 cup dry red wine
- 1 onion, sliced
- 4 carrots, cut into chunks
- 1 tablespoon olive oil
- Pepper and salt to taste

DIRECTIONS:

1. Add oil into the instant pot and set the pot on sauté mode.
2. Add meat and sauté until brown. Add onion and sauté until softened.
3. Add the remaining ingredients and stir well.
4. Seal pot with lid and cook on high for 12 minutes.
5. Once done, allow releasing pressure naturally. Remove the lid.
6. Stir well and serve.

NUTRITION: Calories: 744 Fat: 51.3g Carbohydrates: 14.5g Sugar: 6.5g Protein: 48.1g Cholesterol: 175mg

Delicious Beef Chili

Preparation time: 10 minutes.
Level: Average.
Cooking time: 35 minutes.
Serving: 4

INGREDIENTS:

- 2 pounds ground beef
- 1 teaspoon olive oil
- 1 teaspoon garlic, minced
- 1 small onion, chopped
- 2 tablespoons chili powder
- 1 teaspoon oregano
- 1/2 teaspoon thyme
- 28 ounces can tomato, crushed
- 2 cups beef stock
- 2 carrots, chopped
- 3 sweet potatoes, peeled and cubed
- Pepper and salt to taste

DIRECTIONS:

1. Add oil into the instant pot and set the pot on sauté mode.
2. Add meat and cook until brown.
3. Add the remaining ingredients and stir well.
4. Seal pot with the lid and cook on high for 35 minutes.
5. Once done, allow releasing pressure naturally. Remove the lid.
6. Stir well and serve.

NUTRITION: Calories: 302 Fat: 8.2g Carbohydrates: 19.2g Sugar: 4.8g Protein: 37.1g Cholesterol: 101mg

Basic Meatballs

Preparation time: 15 minutes.
Level: Easy.
Cooking time: 15 minutes.
Servings: 4
INGREDIENTS:

- 1 pound 90% lean ground beef
- 1 onion, finely chopped
- 1 garlic clove, minced
- 1 large egg, beaten
- ¼ cup homemade bread crumbs or store-bought unseasoned bread crumbs
- 1 tablespoon Italian seasoning
- ½ teaspoon salt
- ¼ teaspoon freshly ground black pepper
- 2 tablespoons olive oil

DIRECTIONS:

1. In a large bowl, combine the ground beef, onion, garlic, egg, bread crumbs, Italian seasoning, salt, and pepper. Use clean hands to mix until well blended.
2. Shape 1 tablespoon of the meatball mixture into a ball, and place it on a large plate. Repeat with the remaining mixture to make about 20 meatballs.
3. In a large skillet over medium heat, heat the olive oil. When the oil is shimmering, add the meatballs and cook, covered for about 15 minutes browning on all sides until a thermometer inserted into a meatball reads 155°F.
4. Serve warm or freeze for later. To freeze, store cooled meatballs in a freezer-safe container in the freezer for up to 2 months. To defrost, refrigerate overnight. Reheat meatballs in a saucepan along with some Basic Tomato Sauce: Bring the sauce to a boil, then lower and simmer for 10 to 15 minutes until the meatballs are warmed through. Single-serve portions can be reheated in the microwave on high for about 2 minutes.

NUTRITION: Calories: 269 Total fat: 15g Saturated fat: 5g Protein: 26g Carbohydrates: 6g Fiber: 1g Sodium: 427mg

Olive and Feta Burgers

Preparation time: 15 minutes.
Level: Easy.
Cooking time: 15 minutes.
Servings: 4
INGREDIENTS:

- 1 pound 90% lean ground beef
- ½ cup crumbled feta cheese
- ½ cup pitted Kalamata olives, chopped
- 1 garlic clove, minced
- 1 large egg, beaten
- ¼ cup homemade bread crumbs or store-bought unseasoned bread crumbs
- ¼ teaspoon freshly ground black pepper
- 2 tablespoons olive oil

DIRECTIONS:

1. In a large bowl, combine the ground beef, feta, olives, garlic, egg, bread crumbs, and pepper.
2. Use clean hands to evenly divide the mixture into 4 burger patties. In a large skillet or grill pan over medium-high heat, heat the olive oil. When the oil is shimmering, add the patties and cook for 3 to 5 minutes on each side, until browned and cooked through.

NUTRITION: Calories: 325 Total fat: 21g Saturated fat: 8g Protein: 28g Carbohydrates: 5g Fiber: 1g Sodium: 388mg

Meatloaf in a Pinch

Preparation time: 15 minutes.
Level: Difficult.
Cooking time: 1 hour.
Servings: 4

INGREDIENTS:

- Cooking spray
- 1(½) pound 90% lean ground beef
- 1 cup homemade barbecue sauce or store-bought barbecue sauce, divided
- ¾ cup quick-cooking oats
- 1 onion, finely chopped
- 1 garlic clove, minced
- 1 large egg, beaten
- ½ teaspoon salt
- ¼ teaspoon freshly ground black pepper

DIRECTIONS:

1. Preheat the oven to 350°F. Coat a 9-by-5-inch loaf pan with cooking spray.
2. In a large bowl, add the ground beef, ½ cup of barbecue sauce, and the oats, onion, garlic, egg, salt, and pepper. Use clean hands to mix until well combined.
3. Place the meat mixture into the prepared loaf pan, making sure the top is level. Pour the remaining ½ cup of barbecue sauce over the meatloaf, using a spatula or the back of a wooden spoon to evenly spread it.
4. Bake for about 1 hour, until a thermometer inserted into the center of the meatloaf reads 155°F.
5. Remove from the oven, and allow cooling for 10 minutes. Cut into 8 equal slices.
6. Serve warm or freeze for later. To freeze, store cooled meatloaf sliced in a freezer-safe container in the freezer for up to 2 months. To defrost, refrigerate overnight. Reheat individual portions in the microwave on high for 1 to 1(½) minute.

NUTRITION: Calories: 244 Total fat: 10g Saturated fat: 4g Protein: 19g Carbohydrates: 18g Fiber: 1g Sodium: 546mg

Skirt Steak Fajitas

Preparation time: 15 minutes, plus 30 minutes to marinate.
Level: Easy.
Cooking time: 15 minutes.
Servings: 4
INGREDIENTS:

- 2 tablespoons olive oil
- 1 garlic clove, minced
- 1(½) teaspoons smoked paprika
- ½ teaspoon ground cumin
- ½ teaspoon salt, divided
- ¼ teaspoon freshly ground black pepper, divided
- 1(¼) pound skirt steak
- Cooking spray
- 2 yellow bell peppers, seeded and cut into ¼-inch strips
- 1 large onion, thinly sliced

DIRECTIONS:

1. In a large bowl, whisk the olive oil, garlic, paprika, cumin, ¼ teaspoon of salt, and 1/8 teaspoon of pepper. Add the skirt steak and toss to evenly coat. Cover the bowl and marinate in the refrigerator for at least 30 minutes and up to overnight.
2. Coat a large grill pan with cooking spray and heat over medium-high heat. Add the skirt steak and cook for 8 to 12 minutes, turning once, until it reaches an internal cooking temperature of 145°F.
3. Remove the steak from the grill pan and transfer to a cutting board to cool for 5 minutes.
4. Coat the grill pan again with cooking spray. Add the peppers and onion, and cook for about 5 minutes, until the vegetables soften.
5. Meanwhile, cut the steak into 1-inch strips.
6. Add the steak strips and the remaining ¼ teaspoon of salt and the remaining 1/8 teaspoon of pepper to the pan with the vegetables, and toss to combine.
7. Serve warm or freeze for later. To freeze, place cooled meat and vegetables in a resalable container in the freezer for up to 2 months. To defrost, refrigerate overnight. Reheat on the stove-top over medium heat for 8 to 10 minutes, until heated through. Individual portions can be reheated in the microwave on high for 1(½) to 2 minutes.

NUTRITION: Calories: 367 Total fat: 25g Saturated fat: 8g Protein: 30g Carbohydrates: 7g Fiber: 2g Sodium: 355mg

Grilled Steak with Herb Sauce

Preparation time: 10 minutes.
Level: Average.
Cooking time: 20 minutes.
Servings: 4

INGREDIENTS:

- Cooking spray
- 1 (1(¼)-pound) sirloin steak
- ½ teaspoon salt
- 1/8 teaspoon freshly ground black pepper
- 1 cup roughly chopped fresh cilantro leaves and stems
- 2 tablespoons capers, drained
- 2 scallions, roughly chopped
- 2 tablespoons olive oil
- ¼ cup water
- Juice of 1 lemon
- 1 garlic clove, minced

DIRECTIONS:

1. Preheat the oven to 400°F. Coat an oven-proof grill pan or skillet with cooking spray.
2. Sprinkle both sides of the steak with salt and pepper.
3. Heat the prepared grill pan over high heat. When the pan is hot, add the steak and cook on each side for 2 minutes. Place the pan in the oven and roast for about 12 minutes until the steak reaches an internal temperature of 145°F.
4. Remove from the oven and transfer the steak to a cutting board to rest for 5 minutes.
5. Meanwhile, in a blender, add the cilantro, capers, scallions, olive oil, water, lemon juice, and garlic, and blend until almost smooth but still a little chunky.
6. Thinly slice the steak, and serve with the herb sauce.

NUTRITION: Calories: 335 Total fat: 23g Saturated fat: 7g Protein: 30g Carbohydrates: 2g Fiber: 0g Sodium: 493mg

Beef Tenderloin with Red Wine Reduction

Preparation time: 10 minutes.
Level: Average.
Cooking time: 30 minutes.
Servings: 4
INGREDIENTS:

- Cooking spray
- 4 (5-ounce) beef tenderloin steaks
- ½ teaspoon salt, divided
- ¼ teaspoon freshly ground black pepper, divided
- 1 cup dry red wine
- 1 shallot, finely chopped
- 1 tablespoon tomato paste
- ½ cup low-sodium beef broth

DIRECTIONS:

1. Coat a grill pan with cooking spray and heat over medium heat.
2. Sprinkle the steaks with ¼ teaspoon of salt and 1/8 teaspoon of pepper.
3. When the cooking spray is shimmering, place the steaks in the pan and cook for 7 to 10 minutes, turning once, until a thermometer inserted into the thickest part reads 145°F. Transfer the steaks to a platter.
4. In a small saucepan, add the wine, shallot, and tomato paste, and bring to a boil. Reduce heat and simmer for 8 minutes, stirring occasionally, until the liquid is reduced by about half. Add the beef broth and return the mixture to a boil. Reduce heat and simmer for another 8 minutes until the liquid is again reduced by about half. Add the remaining ¼ teaspoon of salt and the remaining 1/8 teaspoon of pepper, and stir to combine.
5. Top each steak with 3 tablespoons of red wine reduction.

NUTRITION: Calories: 230 Total fat: 10g Saturated fat: 4g Protein: 31g Carbohydrates: 3g Fiber: 1g Sodium: 425mg

Slow Cooker Shredded Barbecue Beef

Preparation time: 15 minutes.
Level: Difficult.
Cooking time: 6 to 8 hours.
Servings: 4

INGREDIENTS:

- 1 (4-pound) pot roast, like bottom round
- ½ cup Homemade Barbecue Sauce or bottled barbecue sauce
- ½ cup low-sodium beef broth

DIRECTIONS:

1. Place the pot roast in a slow cooker and cover with the barbecue sauce and beef broth. Using the back of a wooden spoon or spatula, spread the barbecue sauce over the pot roast. Cover and cook on low for 6 to 8 hours, until a thermometer inserted into the center of the roast reads 145°F.
2. Remove the roast and transfer to a plate, reserving the sauce. Allow the roast to cool for 10 minutes.
3. Using two forks, shred the beef and place it into a large bowl. Add the reserved sauce and toss to coat.
4. Serve warm or freeze for later. To freeze, store cooled beef in a freezer-safe container in the freezer for up to 2 months. To defrost, refrigerate overnight. Reheat in a saucepan over medium heat for 5 to 10 minutes until the beef and sauce are warmed through. Single-serve portions can be reheated in the microwave on high for about 1(½) minutes.

NUTRITION: Calories: 434 Total fat: 13g Saturated fat: 5g Protein: 67g Carbohydrates: 8g Fiber: 0g Sodium: 464mg

Slow Cooker Beef with Bell Peppers

Preparation time: 10 minutes.
Level: Difficult.
Cooking time: 6 to 8 hours.
Servings: 4
INGREDIENTS:

- 1(2-pound) top round steak or London broil
- ½ teaspoon salt
- ¼ teaspoon freshly ground black pepper
- 1 large onion, thinly sliced
- 2 red bell peppers, seeded and cut into ¼-inch strips
- ¾ cup basic tomato sauce or jarred tomato sauce
- ½ cup low-sodium beef broth

DIRECTIONS:

1. Season the steak with salt and pepper, and place in the slow cooker. Top with the onion, peppers, tomato sauce, and broth. Stir to combine. Cover and cook on low for 6 to 8 hours, until the beef reaches an internal cooking temperature of 145°F.
2. Cut the steak into thin slices and serve warm or freeze for later. To freeze, place cooled steak with vegetables and liquid into a resealable container in the freezer for up to 2 months. To defrost, refrigerate overnight. Reheat in a large skillet on the stovetop for about 10 minutes, or reheat individual portions in the microwave on high for about 2 minutes.

NUTRITION: Calories: 248 Total fat: 9g Saturated fat: 3g Protein: 34g Carbohydrates: 6g Fiber: 2g Sodium: 386mg

Herbed Pork Meatballs

Preparation time: 15 minutes.
Level: Easy.
Cooking time: 15 minutes.
Servings: 4
INGREDIENTS:

- 1-pound ground pork
- 1 onion, finely chopped
- 1 garlic clove, minced
- 1 large egg, beaten
- ½ cup whole-wheat panko bread crumbs
- ½ cup finely chopped fresh parsley
- ½ teaspoon salt
- ¼ teaspoon freshly ground black pepper
- 2 tablespoons olive oil

DIRECTIONS:

1. In a large bowl, combine the ground pork, onion, garlic, egg, bread crumbs, parsley, salt, and pepper.
2. Shape 1 tablespoon of the pork mixture into a ball, and place it on a large plate. Repeat with the remaining mixture to make about 20 meatballs.
3. In a large skillet over medium heat, heat the olive oil. When the oil is shimmering, add the meatballs and cook, covered, for about 15 minutes, browning on all sides until a thermometer inserted into a meatball reads 155°F.
4. Serve warm or freeze for later. To freeze, store cooled meatballs in a resalable container in the freezer for up to 2 months. To defrost, refrigerate overnight. Reheat the meatballs in a saucepan along with Basic Tomato Sauce: Bring the sauce to a boil, then lower and simmer for 10 to 15 minutes until the meatballs are warmed through. Single-serve portions of meatballs can be reheated in the microwave on high for about 2 minutes.

NUTRITION: Calories: 365 Total fat: 26g Saturated fat: 7g Protein: 23g Carbohydrates: 9g Fiber: 1g Sodium: 406mg

Pork Tenderloin with Apple-Tarragon Sauce

Preparation time: 5 minutes.
Level: Average.
Cooking time: 25 minutes.
Servings: 4
INGREDIENTS:

- 1 tablespoon olive oil
- 1 (1¼-pound) pork tenderloin
- 2 medium apples, cored and sliced
- 1 tablespoon unsalted butter
- 2 garlic cloves, minced
- 2 cups apple cider vinegar
- ½ teaspoon salt
- 1/8 teaspoon freshly ground black pepper
- 2 teaspoons chopped fresh tarragon

DIRECTIONS:

1. Preheat the oven to 400°F.
2. In a large oven-proof skillet over medium heat, heat the olive oil. When the oil is shimmering, add the pork tenderloin and cook for about 8 minutes, turning occasionally, until browned on all sides.
3. Add the apple slices, and place the skillet in the oven. Bake for about 20 minutes, until the pork reaches a minimum internal temperature of 145°F. Place the pork on a cutting board to cool for 5 minutes. Transfer the apples to a plate, and set them aside.
4. Carefully return the skillet to the stovetop over medium heat and add the butter. When the butter is melted, add the garlic and cook until fragrant, 1 minute. Add the apple cider vinegar, and use a wooden spoon to scrape the pork bits from the bottom of the pan. Bring the mixture to a boil, then reduce heat and simmer for 2 minutes, until the flavors combine. Add the salt, pepper, and tarragon, and stir to incorporate. Turn off the heat.
5. Thinly slice the cooled pork tenderloin, then return it to the skillet. Add the apples and toss to coat. Transfer to a serving dish and serve warm.

NUTRITION: Calories: 256 Total fat: 9g Saturated fat: 3g Protein: 29g Carbohydrates: 13g Fiber: 2g Sodium: 641 mg

Miso-Garlic Pork Chops

Preparation time: 10 minutes, plus 30 minutes to marinate.
Level: Easy.
Cooking time: 10 minutes.
Servings: 4
INGREDIENTS:

- 1/3 cup white miso
- 1/3 cup sake
- 1/3 cup mirin
- 2 teaspoons minced fresh ginger
- 1 garlic clove, minced
- 4 (5-ounce) boneless pork loin chops
- Cooking spray
- 1 tablespoon olive oil

DIRECTIONS:

1. In a large bowl, mix the miso, sake, mirin, ginger, and garlic into a smooth paste.
2. Add the pork chops and turn to coat all sides with the glaze. Marinate in the refrigerator for at least 30 minutes or up to overnight.
3. Coat a grill pan with cooking spray and heat over medium heat. Alternatively, brush the grates of an outdoor grill with olive oil. When the pan or grill is hot, cook the pork chops for about 3 to 5 minutes on each side, until they reach an internal cooking temperature of 145°F.

NUTRITION: Calories: 209 Total fat: 4g Saturated fat: 1g Protein: 32g Carbohydrates: 12g Fiber: 1g Sodium: 932mg

Slow Cooker Honey Mustard Pork with Pears

Preparation time: 10 minutes.
Level: Difficult.
Cooking time: 3 to 4 hours on high for 6 to 8 hours on low.
Servings: 4
INGREDIENTS:

- ¼ cup homemade honey mustard
- 1/3 cup low-sodium chicken broth
- ½ teaspoon salt
- ¼ teaspoon freshly ground black pepper
- 1 (2-pound) boneless pork loin, fat trimmed
- 2 pears, peeled, cored, and thinly sliced
- 1 tablespoon cornstarch
- 2 tablespoons water

DIRECTIONS:

1. In a small bowl, whisk together the honey mustard, broth, salt, and pepper.
2. Place the pork and pears in the slow cooker. Pour the honey mustard mixture over the top.
3. Cover and cook on high for 3 to 4 hours or on low for 6 to 8 hours.
4. Remove the pork from the slow cooker, retaining the pears and liquid, and transfer to a cutting board to cool for 10 minutes, then thinly slice.
5. In a small bowl, whisk together the cornstarch and water.
6. In a medium skillet over medium heat, heat the pears and liquid from the slow cooker. Add the cornstarch mixture and continue whisking for about 3 minutes, until the mixture thickens.
7. Serve the pork slices topped with the warm sauce, or freeze for later. To freeze, store cooled pork in a freezer-safe container in the freezer for up to 2 months. To defrost, refrigerate overnight. Reheat in a saucepan over medium heat for 5 to 10 minutes, until the pork and sauce are warmed through. Single-serve portions can be reheated in the microwave on high for about 1(½) minutes.

NUTRITION: Calories: 212 Total fat: 8g Saturated fat: 2g Protein: 24g Carbohydrates: 9g Fiber: 1g Sodium: 368mg

Slow Cooker Cranberry Pork Chops

Preparation time: 10 minutes.
Level: Difficult.
Cooking time: 3 hours on high or 6 hours on low.
Servings: 4
INGREDIENTS:

- 4 (5-ounce) boneless pork chops
- ½ teaspoon salt
- ¼ teaspoon freshly ground black pepper
- 1 onion, thinly sliced
- 1(½) cups fresh or thawed frozen cranberries
- ½ cup apple juice
- ¼ cup balsamic vinegar
- 2 tablespoons honey

DIRECTIONS:

1. Season both sides of the pork chops with salt and pepper.
2. In a slow cooker, add the pork chops, onion, and cranberries.
3. In a small bowl, whisk together the apple juice, balsamic vinegar, and honey. Pour over the pork chops.
4. Cover and cook on high for 3 hours or on low for 6 hours.
5. Serve warm or freeze for later. To freeze, store cooled pork chops with the sauce in a freezer-safe container in the freezer for up to 2 months. To defrost, refrigerate overnight. Reheat the pork chops and sauce in a saucepan over medium-high heat for about 10 minutes. Alternatively, reheat individual pork chops with sauce in the microwave on high for about 2 minutes.

NUTRITION: Calories: 278 Total fat: 10g Saturated fat: 3g Protein: 24g Carbohydrates: 21g Fiber: 2g Sodium: 361 mg

Chicken and Olives

Preparation time: 10 minutes.
Level: Easy.
Cooking time: 15 minutes.
Servings: 4
INGREDIENTS:

- 4 chicken breasts, skinless and boneless
- 2 tablespoons garlic, minced
- 1 tablespoon oregano, dried
- Salt and black pepper to taste
- 2 tablespoons olive oil
- ½ cup chicken stock
- Juice of 1 lemon
- 1 cup red onion, chopped
- 1(½) cup tomatoes, cubed
- ¼ cup green olives, pitted and sliced
- A handful of parsley, chopped

DIRECTIONS:

1. Heat up a pan with the oil over medium-high heat, add the chicken, garlic, salt, pepper, and brown for 2 minutes on each side.
2. Add the rest of the ingredients, toss, bring the mix to a simmer and cook over medium heat for 13 minutes.
3. Divide the mix between plates and serve.

NUTRITION: Calories: 135 Fat: 5.8g Fiber: 3.4g Carbs: 12.1g Protein: 9.6g

Chicken Bake

Preparation time: 10 minutes.
Level: Average.
Cooking time: 30 minutes.
Servings: 4
INGREDIENTS:

- 1(½) pound chicken thighs, skinless, boneless, and cubed
- 2 garlic cloves, minced
- 1 tablespoon oregano, chopped
- 2 tablespoons olive oil
- 1 tablespoon red wine vinegar
- ½ cup canned artichokes, drained and chopped
- 1 red onion, sliced
- 1-pound whole-wheat fusilli pasta, cooked
- ½ cup canned white beans, drained and rinsed
- ½ cup parsley, chopped
- 1 cup mozzarella, shredded
- Salt and black pepper to taste

DIRECTIONS:

1. Heat up a pan with half of the oil over medium-high heat, add the meat, and brown for 5 minutes.
2. Grease a baking pan with the rest of the oil, add the browned chicken, and the rest of the ingredients except the pasta and the mozzarella.
3. Spread the pasta all over and toss gently.
4. Sprinkle the mozzarella on top and bake at 425°F for 25 minutes.
5. Divide the bake between plates and serve.

NUTRITION: Calories: 195 Fat: 5.8g Fiber: 3.4g Carbs: 12.1g Protein: 11.6g

Chicken and Artichokes

Preparation time: 10 minutes.
Level: Average.
Cooking time: 20 minutes.
Servings: 4
INGREDIENTS:

- 2 pounds chicken breast, skinless, boneless, and sliced
- A pinch of salt and black pepper
- 4 tablespoons olive oil
- 8 ounces canned roasted artichoke hearts, drained
- 6 ounces sun-dried tomatoes, chopped
- 3 tablespoons capers, drained
- 2 tablespoons lemon juice

DIRECTIONS:

1. Heat up a pan with half of the oil over medium-high heat, add the artichokes and the other ingredients except the chicken, stir and sauté for 10 minutes.
2. Transfer the mix to a bowl, heat up the pan again with the rest of the oil over medium-high heat, add the meat and cook for 4 minutes on each side.
3. Return the veggie mix to the pan, toss, cook everything for 2-3 minutes more, divide between plates, and serve.

NUTRITION: Calories: 552 Fat: 28g Fiber: 6g Carbs: 33g Protein: 43g

Chicken Kebabs

Preparation time: 30 minutes.
Level: Average.
Cooking time: 20 minutes.
Servings: 4
INGREDIENTS:

- 2 chicken breasts, skinless, boneless, and cubed
- 1 red bell pepper, cut into squares
- 1 red onion, roughly cut into squares
- 2 teaspoons sweet paprika
- 1 teaspoon nutmeg, ground
- 1 teaspoon Italian seasoning
- ¼ teaspoon smoked paprika
- A pinch of salt and black pepper
- ¼ teaspoon cardamom, ground
- Juice of 1 lemon
- 3 garlic cloves, minced
- ½ cup olive oil

DIRECTIONS:

1. In a bowl, combine the chicken with the onion, the bell pepper, and the other ingredients, toss well, cover the bowl and keep in the fridge for 30 minutes.
2. Assemble skewers with chicken, peppers, and onions, place them on your preheated grill and cook over medium heat for 8 minutes on each side.
3. Divide the kebabs between plates and serve with a side salad.

NUTRITION: Calories: 262 Fat: 14g Fiber: 2g Carbs: 14g Protein: 20g

Chili Chicken Mix

Preparation time: 10 minutes.
Level: Average.
Cooking time: 18 minutes.
Servings: 4
INGREDIENTS:

- 2 pounds chicken thighs, skinless and boneless
- 2 tablespoons olive oil
- 2 cups yellow onion, chopped
- 1 teaspoon onion powder
- 1 teaspoon smoked paprika
- 1 teaspoon chili pepper
- ½ teaspoon coriander seeds, ground
- 2 teaspoons oregano, dried
- 2 teaspoon parsley flakes
- 30 ounces canned tomatoes, chopped
- ½ cup black olives, pitted and halved

DIRECTIONS:

1. Set the instant pot on sauté mode, add the oil, heat it up, add the onion, onion powder, and the rest of the ingredients except the tomatoes, olives, and the chicken, stir and sauté for 10 minutes.
2. Add the chicken, tomatoes, and olives, put the lid on, and cook on high for 8 minutes.
3. Release the pressure naturally for 10 minutes, divide the mix into bowls and serve.

NUTRITION: Calories: 153 Fat: 8g Fiber: 2g Carbs: 9g Protein: 12g

Chicken Pilaf

Preparation time: 10 minutes.
Level: Average.
Cooking time: 30 minutes.
Servings: 4
INGREDIENTS:

- 4 tablespoons avocado oil
- 2 pounds chicken breasts, skinless, boneless, and cubed
- ½ cup yellow onion, chopped
- 4 garlic cloves, minced
- 8 ounces brown rice
- 4 cups chicken stock
- ½ cup kalamata olives, pitted
- ½ cup tomatoes, cubed
- 6 ounces baby spinach
- ½ cup feta cheese, crumbled
- A pinch of salt and black pepper
- 1 tablespoon marjoram, chopped
- 1 tablespoon basil, chopped
- Juice of ½ lemon
- ¼ cup pine nuts, toasted

DIRECTIONS:

1. Heat up a pot with 1 tablespoon avocado oil over medium-high heat, add the chicken, some salt, and pepper, brown for 5 minutes on each side, and transfer to a bowl.
2. Heat up the pot again with the rest of the avocado oil over medium heat, add the onion and garlic and sauté for 3 minutes.
3. Add the rice, the rest of the ingredients except the pine nuts, also return the chicken, toss, bring to a simmer and cook over medium heat for 20 minutes.
4. Divide the mix between plates, top each serving with some pine nuts and serve.

NUTRITION: Calories: 283 Fat: 12.5g Fiber: 8.2g Carbs: 21.5g Protein: 13.4g

Chapter 10:
EGG, OMELETTE, AND SAUCE DISHES

<u>Mediterranean Egg Muffins with Ham</u>

Preparation time: 15 minutes.
Level: Average.
Cooking time: 15 minutes.
Servings: 4
INGREDIENTS:

- 9 slices of thin cut deli ham
- 1/2 cup canned roasted red pepper, sliced + additional for garnish
- 1/3 cup fresh spinach, minced
- 1/4 cup feta cheese, crumbled
- 5 large eggs
- Pinch of salt
- Pinch of pepper
- 1 1/2 tablespoons pesto sauce
- Fresh basil for garnish

DIRECTIONS:

1. Preheat the oven to 400°F. Spray a muffin tin with cooking spray, generously. Line each of the muffin tin with 1(½) pieces of ham—making sure there aren't any holes for the egg mixture to come out.
2. Place some of the roasted red pepper in the bottom of each muffin tin. Place 1 tablespoon of minced spinach on top of each red pepper. Top the pepper and spinach off with a large 1/2 tablespoon of crumbled feta cheese.
3. In a medium bowl, whisk together the eggs salt, and pepper, divide the egg mixture evenly among the 6 muffin tins.
4. Bake for 15 to 17 minutes until the eggs are puffy and set. Remove each cup from the muffin tin. Allow cooling completely.
5. Distribute the muffins among the containers, store them in the fridge for 2–3 days or in the freezer for 3 months.

NUTRITION: Calories: 109 Carbs: 2g Fat: 6g Protein: 9g

Sun-Dried Tomatoes, Dill, and Feta Omelet Casserole

Preparation time: 15 minutes.
Level: Difficult.
Cooking time: 40 minutes.
Servings: 4
INGREDIENTS:

- 12 large eggs
- 2 cups whole milk
- 8 ounces fresh spinach
- 2 cloves garlic, minced
- 12 ounces artichoke salad with olives and peppers, drained and chopped
- 5 ounces sun-dried tomato
- 5 ounces feta cheese, crumbled
- 1 tablespoon fresh chopped dill or 1 teaspoon dried dill
- 1 teaspoon dried oregano
- 1 teaspoon lemon-pepper
- 1 teaspoon salt
- 4 teaspoons olive oil, divided

DIRECTIONS:

1. Preheat the oven to 375°F. Chop the fresh herbs and artichoke salad. In a skillet over medium heat, add 1 tablespoon of olive oil.
2. Sauté the spinach and garlic until wilted for about 3 minutes. Oil a 9x13 inch baking dish, layer the spinach and artichoke salad evenly in the dish.
3. In a medium bowl, whisk together the eggs, milk, herbs, salt, and lemon-pepper. Pour the egg mixture over vegetables, sprinkle with feta cheese.
4. Bake in the center of the oven for 35–40 minutes until firm in the center. Allow cooling, slice, and distribute among the storage containers. Store for 2–3 days or freeze for 3 months.

NUTRITION: Calories: 196 Carbohydrates: 5g Fat: 12g Protein: 10g

Breakfast Taco Scramble

Preparation time: 15 minutes.
Level: Difficult.
Cooking time: 1 hour & 25 minutes.
Servings: 4
INGREDIENTS:

- 8 large eggs, beaten
- 1/4 teaspoons seasoning salt
- 1 pound 99% lean ground turkey
- 2 tablespoons Greek seasoning
- 1/2 small onion, minced
- 2 tablespoons bell pepper, minced
- 4 ounces can tomato sauce
- 1/4 cup water

For the potatoes:

- 12 (1 pound) baby gold or red potatoes, quartered
- 4 teaspoons olive oil
- 3/4 teaspoons salt
- 1/2 teaspoons garlic powder
- Fresh black pepper, to taste

DIRECTIONS:

1. In a large bowl, beat the eggs, season with seasoning salt. Preheat the oven to 425°F. Spray a 9x12 or large oval casserole dish with cooking oil.
2. Add the potatoes, 1 tablespoon of oil, 3/4 teaspoon of salt, garlic powder, and black pepper, and toss to coat. Bake for 45 minutes to 1 hour, tossing every 15 minutes.
3. In the meantime, brown the turkey in a large skillet over medium heat, breaking it up while it cooks. Once no longer pink, add in the Greek seasoning.
4. Add in the bell pepper, onion, tomato sauce, and water, stir and cover, simmer on low for about 20 minutes. Spray a different skillet with nonstick spray over medium heat.
5. Once heated, add in the eggs seasoned with 1/4 teaspoons of salt and scramble for 2–3 minutes, or cook until it sets.
6. Distribute 3/4 cup turkey and 2/3 cup eggs and divide the potatoes in each storage container, store for 3-4 days.

NUTRITION: Calories: 450 Fat: 19g Carbs: 24.5g Protein: 46g

Mediterranean Quinoa and Feta Egg Muffins

Preparation time: 15 minutes.
Level: Average.
Cooking time: 30 minutes.
Servings: 4
INGREDIENTS:

- 8 eggs
- 1 cup cooked quinoa
- 1 cup crumbled feta cheese
- 1/4 teaspoons salt
- 2 cups baby spinach finely chopped
- 1/2 cup finely chopped onion
- 1 cup chopped or sliced tomatoes, cherry or grape tomatoes
- 1/2 cup chopped and pitted kalamata olives
- 1 tablespoon chopped fresh oregano
- 2 teaspoons high oleic sunflower oil plus optional extra for greasing muffin tins

DIRECTIONS:

1. Pre-heat oven to 350°F. Prepare 12 silicone muffin holders on a baking sheet, or grease a 12-cup muffin tin with oil, set aside.
2. In a skillet over medium heat, add the vegetable oil and onions, sauté for 2 minutes. Add tomatoes, sauté for another minute, then add spinach and sauté until wilted for about 1 minute.
3. Remove from heat and stir in olives and oregano, set aside. Place the eggs in a blender or mixing bowl and blend or mix until well combined.
4. Pour the eggs into a mixing bowl (if you use a blender) then add quinoa, feta cheese, veggie mixture, and salt, and stir until well combined.
5. Pour mixture into silicone cups or greased muffin tins, dividing equally, and bake for 30 minutes, or until eggs have set and muffins are a light golden brown. Allow cooling completely.

NUTRITION: Calories: 113 Carbohydrates: 5g Fat: 7g Protein: 6g

Eggs, Mint, and Tomatoes

Preparation time: 10 minutes.
Level: Easy.
Cooking time: 15 minutes.
Servings: 4
INGREDIENTS:

- 2 eggs, whisked
- 2 tomatoes, cubed
- 2 teaspoons olive oil
- 1 tablespoon mint, chopped
- 1 tablespoon chives, chopped
- Salt and black pepper to taste

DIRECTIONS:

1. Heat up a pan with the oil over medium heat, add the tomatoes and the rest of the ingredients except the eggs, stir and cook for 5 minutes.
2. Add the eggs, toss, cook for 10 minutes more, divide between plates and serve.

NUTRITION: Calories: 300 Fat: 15.3g Fiber: 4.5g Carbs: 17.7g Protein: 11g

Cottage Cheese and Berries Omelet

Preparation time: 5 minutes.
Level: Easy.
Cooking time: 4 minutes.
Servings: 4
INGREDIENTS:

- 1 egg, whisked
- ½ teaspoon olive oil
- 1 teaspoon cinnamon powder
- 1 tablespoon almond milk
- 3 ounces cottage cheese
- 4 ounces blueberries

DIRECTIONS:

1. In a bowl, mix the egg with the rest of the ingredients except the oil and toss.
2. Heat up a pan with the oil over medium heat, add the eggs and mix, spread, cook for 2 minutes on each side, transfer to a plate and serve.

NUTRITION: Calories: 221 Fat: 10.3g Fiber: 7.4g Carbohydrates: 3.3g Protein: 9.1g

Salmon Frittata

Preparation time: 5 minutes.
Level: Average.
Cooking time: 27 minutes.
Servings: 4
INGREDIENTS:

- 1-pound gold potatoes, roughly cubed
- 1 tablespoon olive oil
- Cooking spray
- 2 salmon fillets, skinless and boneless
- 8 eggs, whisked
- 1 teaspoon mint, chopped
- A pinch of salt and black pepper

DIRECTIONS:

1. Put the potatoes in a pot, add water to cover, bring to a boil over medium heat, cook for 12 minutes, drain and transfer to a bowl.
2. Arrange the salmon on a baking sheet lined with parchment paper, grease with cooking spray, and broil over medium-high heat for 5 minutes on each side, cool down, flake, and put in a separate bowl.
3. Heat up a pan with the oil over medium heat, add the potatoes, salmon, and the rest of the ingredients except the eggs, and toss.
4. Add the eggs on top, put the lid on and cook over medium heat for 10 minutes.
5. Divide the salmon between plates and serve.

NUTRITION: Calories: 311 Fat: 11.2g Fiber: 8.2g Carbohydrates: 4.4g Protein: 10.2g

Lentils and Cheddar Frittata

Preparation time: 10 minutes.
Level: Easy.
Cooking time: 15 minutes.
Servings: 4

INGREDIENTS:
- 1 red onion, chopped
- 2 tablespoons olive oil
- 1 cup sweet potatoes, boiled and chopped
- ¾ cup ham, chopped
- 4 eggs, whisked
- ¾ cup lentils, cooked
- 2 tablespoons Greek yogurt
- Salt and black pepper to taste
- ½ cup cherry tomatoes, halved
- ¾ cup cheddar cheese, grated

DIRECTIONS:
1. Heat up a pan with the oil over medium heat, add the onion, stir and sauté for 2 minutes.
2. Add the rest of the ingredients except the eggs and the cheese, toss and cook for 3 minutes more.
3. Add the eggs, sprinkle the cheese on top, cover the pan and cook for 10 minutes more.
4. Slice the frittata, divide between plates and serve.

NUTRITION: Calories: 322 Fat: 9.3g Fiber: 9.4g Carbohydrates: 5.3g Protein: 8.1g

Cheesy Eggs Ramekins

Preparation time: 10 minutes.
Level: Easy.
Cooking time: 10 minutes.
Servings: 4
INGREDIENTS:

- 1 tablespoon chives, chopped
- 1 tablespoon dill, chopped
- A pinch of salt and black pepper
- 2 tablespoons cheddar cheese, grated
- 1 tomato, chopped
- 2 eggs, whisked
- Cooking spray

DIRECTIONS:

1. In a bowl, mix the eggs with the tomato and the rest of the ingredients except the cooking spray and whisk well.
2. Grease 2 ramekins with the cooking spray, divide the mix into each ramekin, bake at 400°F for 10 minutes and serve.

NUTRITION: Calories: 104 Fat: 7.1g Fiber: 0.6g Carbs: 2.6g Protein: 7.9g

Leeks and Eggs Muffins

Preparation time: 10 minutes.
Level: Average.
Cooking time: 20 minutes.
Servings: 4
INGREDIENTS:

- 3 eggs, whisked
- ¼ cup baby spinach
- 2 tablespoons leeks, chopped
- 4 tablespoons parmesan, grated
- 2 tablespoons almond milk
- Cooking spray
- 1 small red bell pepper, chopped
- Salt and black pepper to taste
- 1 tomato, cubed
- 2 tablespoons cheddar cheese, grated

DIRECTIONS:

1. In a bowl, combine the eggs with the milk, salt, pepper, and the rest of the ingredients except the cooking spray and whisk well.
2. Grease a muffin tin with the cooking spray and divide the eggs mixture in each muffin mold.
3. Bake at 380°F for 20 minutes and serve them for breakfast.

NUTRITION: Calories: 308 Fat: 19.4g Fiber: 1.7g Carbs: 8.7g Protein: 24.4g

Artichokes and Cheese Omelet

Preparation time: 10 minutes.
Level: Easy.
Cooking time: 8 minutes.
Servings: 4
INGREDIENTS:

- 1 teaspoon avocado oil
- 1 tablespoon almond milk
- 2 eggs, whisked
- A pinch of salt and black pepper
- 2 tablespoons tomato, cubed
- 2 tablespoons kalamata olives, pitted and sliced
- 1 artichoke heart, chopped
- 1 tablespoon tomato sauce
- 1 tablespoon feta cheese, crumbled

DIRECTIONS:

1. In a bowl, combine the eggs with the milk, salt, pepper, and the rest of the ingredients except the avocado oil and whisk well. Heat up a pan with the avocado oil over medium-high heat, add the omelet mix, spread into the pan, cook for 4 minutes, flip, cook for 4 minutes more, transfer to a plate, and serve.

NUTRITION: Calories: 303 Fat: 17.7g Fiber: 9.9g Carbs: 21.9g Protein: 18.2g

Quinoa and Eggs Salad

Preparation time: 5 minutes.
Level: Easy.
Cooking time: 0 minutes.
Servings: 4
INGREDIENTS:

- 4 eggs, soft boiled, peeled, and cut into wedges
- 2 cups baby arugula
- 2 cups cherry tomatoes, halved
- 1 cucumber, sliced
- 1 cup quinoa, cooked
- 1 cup almonds, chopped
- 1 avocado, peeled, pitted, and sliced
- 1 tablespoon olive oil
- ½ cup mixed dill and mint, chopped
- A pinch of salt and black pepper
- Juice of 1 lemon

DIRECTIONS:

1. In a large salad bowl, combine the eggs with the arugula and the rest of the ingredients, toss, divide between plates and serve for breakfast.

NUTRITION: Calories: 519 Fat: 32.4g Fiber: 11g Carbs: 43.3g Protein: 19.1g

Baked Omelet Mix

Preparation time: 10 minutes.
Level: Difficult.
Cooking time: 45 minutes.
Servings: 4
INGREDIENTS:

- 12 eggs, whisked
- 8 ounces spinach, chopped
- 2 cups almond milk
- 12 ounces canned artichokes, chopped
- 2 garlic cloves, minced
- 5 ounces feta cheese, crumbled
- 1 tablespoon dill, chopped
- 1 teaspoon oregano, dried
- 1 teaspoon lemon-pepper
- A pinch of salt
- 4 teaspoons olive oil

DIRECTIONS:

1. Heat up a pan with the oil over medium-high heat, add the garlic and the spinach and sauté for 3 minutes.
2. In a baking dish, combine the eggs with the artichokes and the rest of the ingredients.
3. Add the spinach mix as well, toss a bit, bake the mix at 375°F for 40 minutes, divide between plates and serve for breakfast.

NUTRITION: Calories: 186 Fat: 13g Fiber: 1g Carbs: 5g Protein: 10g

Scrambled Eggs

Preparation time: 10 minutes.
Level: Easy.
Cooking time: 10 minutes.
Servings: 4
INGREDIENTS:
- 1 yellow bell pepper, chopped
- 8 cherry tomatoes, cubed
- 2 spring onions, chopped
- 1 tablespoon olive oil
- 1 tablespoon capers, drained
- 2 tablespoons black olives, pitted and sliced
- 4 eggs
- A pinch of salt and black pepper
- ¼ teaspoon oregano, dried
- 1 tablespoon parsley, chopped

DIRECTIONS:
1. Heat up a pan with the oil over medium-high heat, add the bell pepper and spring onions, and sauté for 3 minutes.
2. Add the tomatoes, capers, and olives and sauté for 2 minutes more.
3. Crack the eggs into the pan, add salt, pepper, oregano, and scramble for 5 minutes more.
4. Divide the scramble between plates, sprinkle parsley on top, and serve.

NUTRITION: Calories: 249 Fat: 17g Fiber: 3.2g Carbs: 13.3g Protein: 13.5g

Quinoa and Eggs Pan

Preparation time: 10 minutes.
Level: Average.
Cooking time: 23 minutes.
Servings: 4
INGREDIENTS:

- 4 bacon slices, cooked and crumbled
- A drizzle of olive oil
- 1 small red onion, chopped
- 1 red bell pepper, chopped
- 1 sweet potato, grated
- 1 green bell pepper, chopped
- 2 garlic cloves, minced
- 1 cup white mushrooms, sliced
- ½ cup quinoa
- 1 cup chicken stock
- 4 eggs, fried
- Salt and black pepper to taste

DIRECTIONS:

1. Heat up a pan with the oil over medium-low heat, add onion, garlic, bell peppers, sweet potato, and mushrooms, toss, and sauté for 5 minutes.
2. Add quinoa, toss, and cook for 1 more minute.
3. Add stock, salt, and pepper, stir and cook for 15 minutes.
4. Divide the mix between plates, top each serving with a fried egg, sprinkle some salt, pepper, and crumbled bacon, and serve for breakfast.

NUTRITION: Calories: 304 Fat: 14g Fiber: 3.8g Carbs: 27.5g Protein: 17.8g

Baked Eggs with Avocado and Basil

Preparation time: 15 minutes.
Level: Easy.
Cooking time: 10 minutes.
Servings: 4
INGREDIENTS:

- 4 bell peppers, any color
- 1 tablespoon extra-virgin olive oil
- 8 large eggs
- ¾ teaspoon kosher salt, divided
- ¼ teaspoon freshly ground black pepper, divided
- 1 avocado, peeled, pitted, and diced
- ¼ cup red onion, diced
- ¼ cup fresh basil, chopped
- Juice of ½ lime

DIRECTIONS:

1. Stem and seed bell peppers. Cut 2 (2-inch-thick) rings from each pepper. Chop the remaining bell pepper into small dice and set aside.
2. Heat the olive oil in a large skillet over medium heat. Add 4 bell pepper rings, then crack 1 egg in the middle of each ring.
3. Season with ¼ teaspoon of salt and 1/8 teaspoon of black pepper. Cook until the egg whites are mostly set, but the yolks are still runny for 2 to 3 minutes.
4. Gently flip and cook for 1 additional minute for an over easy. Move the egg–bell pepper rings to a platter or onto plates and repeats with the remaining 4 bell pepper rings.
5. In a medium bowl, combine the avocado, onion, basil, lime juice, reserved diced bell pepper, the remaining ¼ teaspoon kosher salt, and the remaining 1/8 teaspoon black pepper. Divide among the 4 plates.

NUTRITION: Calories: 270 Protein: 15g Fat: 19g Carbs: 12g

Polenta with Sautéed Chard and Fried Eggs

Preparation time: 5 minutes.
Level: Average.
Cooking time: 20 minutes.
Servings: 4
INGREDIENTS:

- 2(½) cups water
- ½ teaspoon kosher salt
- ¾ cups whole-grain cornmeal
- ¼ teaspoon freshly ground black pepper
- 2 tablespoons grated Parmesan cheese
- 1 tablespoon extra-virgin olive oil
- 1 bunch (about 6 ounces) Swiss chard, leaves and stems chopped and separated
- 2 garlic cloves, sliced
- ¼ teaspoon kosher salt
- 1/8 teaspoon freshly ground black pepper
- Lemon juice (optional)
- 1 tablespoon extra-virgin olive oil
- 4 large eggs

DIRECTIONS:

1. For the polenta, bring the water and salt to a boil in a medium saucepan over high heat. Slowly add the cornmeal, whisking constantly.
2. Decrease the heat to low, cover, and cook for 10 to 15 minutes, stirring often to avoid lumps. Stir in the pepper and Parmesan and divide among 4 bowls.
3. For the chard, heat the oil in a large skillet over medium heat. Add the chard stems, garlic, salt, and pepper; sauté for 2 minutes. Add the chard leaves and cook until wilted about 3 to 5 minutes.
4. Add a spritz of lemon juice (if desired), toss together, and divide evenly on top of the polenta.
5. For the eggs, heat the oil in the same large skillet over medium-high heat. Crack each egg into the skillet, taking care not to crowd the skillet and leaving a space between the eggs.
6. Cook until the whites are set and golden around the edges about 2 to 3 minutes. Serve sunny-side up or flip the eggs over carefully and cook 1 minute longer for over easy. Place one egg on top of the polenta and chard in each bowl.

NUTRITION: Calories: 310 Protein: 17g Fat: 18g Carbs: 21g

Smoked Salmon Egg Scramble with Dill and Chives

Preparation time: 5 minutes.
Level: Easy.
Cooking time: 5 minutes.
Servings: 4
INGREDIENTS:

- 4 large eggs
- 1 tablespoon milk
- 1 tablespoon fresh chives, minced
- 1 tablespoon fresh dill, minced
- ¼ teaspoon kosher salt
- 1/8 teaspoon freshly ground black pepper
- 2 teaspoons extra-virgin olive oil
- 2 ounces smoked salmon, thinly sliced

DIRECTIONS:

1. In a large bowl, whisk together the eggs, milk, chives, dill, salt, and pepper. Heat the olive oil in a medium skillet or sauté pan over medium heat.
2. Add the egg mixture and cook for about 3 minutes, stirring occasionally. Add the salmon and cook until the eggs are set but moist for about 1 minute.

NUTRITION: Calories: 325 Protein: 23g Fat: 26g Carbs: 1g

Slow-Cooked Peppers Frittata

Preparation time: 10 minutes.
Level: Difficult.
Cooking time: 3 hours.
Servings: 4
INGREDIENTS:

- ½ cup almond milk
- 8 eggs, whisked
- Salt and black pepper to taste
- 1 teaspoon oregano, dried
- 1(½) cups roasted peppers, chopped
- ½ cup red onion, chopped
- 4 cups baby arugula
- 1 cup goat cheese, crumbled
- Cooking spray

DIRECTIONS:

1. In a bowl, combine the eggs with salt, pepper, and oregano and whisk. Grease your slow cooker with the cooking spray, arrange the peppers and the remaining ingredients inside and pour the egg mixture over them. Put the lid on and cook on Low for 3 hours. Divide the frittata between plates and serve.

NUTRITION: Calories: 259 Protein: 16g Fat: 20g Carbs: 4.4g

Feta Frittata

Preparation time: 15 minutes.
Level: Average.
Cooking time: 25 minutes.
Servings: 4
INGREDIENTS:

- 1 small clove garlic
- 1 green onion
- 2 large eggs
- ½ cup egg substitute
- 4 tablespoons crumbled feta cheese, divided
- 1/3 cup plum tomato
- 4 thin avocado slices
- 2 tablespoons reduced-fat sour cream
- Also needed: 6-inch skillet

DIRECTIONS:

1. Thinly slice/mince the onion, garlic, and tomato. Peel the avocado before slicing. Heat the pan using the medium temperature setting and spritz it with cooking oil.
2. Whisk the egg substitute, eggs, and feta cheese. Add the egg mixture into the pan. Cover and simmer for four to six minutes.
3. Sprinkle it using the rest of the feta cheese and tomato. Cover and continue cooking until the eggs are set or about two to three more minutes.
4. Wait for about five minutes before cutting it into halves. Serve with avocado and sour cream.

NUTRITION: Calories: 460 Carbs: 8g Fat: 37g Protein: 24g

Mushroom Goat Cheese Frittata

Preparation time: 15 minutes.
Level: Average.
Cooking time: 35 minutes.
Servings: 4
INGREDIENTS:

- 1 tablespoon olive oil
- 1 small onion, diced
- 10 ounces cremini or your favorite mushrooms, sliced
- 1 garlic clove, minced
- 10 eggs
- 2/3 cup half and half
- 1/4 cup fresh chives, minced
- 2 teaspoons fresh thyme, minced
- 1/2 teaspoons kosher salt
- 1/2 teaspoons black pepper
- 4 ounces goat cheese

DIRECTIONS:

1. Preheat the oven to 375°F. In an oven-safe skillet or cast-iron pan over medium heat, olive oil. Add in the onion and sauté for 3–5 minutes until golden.
2. Add in the sliced mushrooms and garlic, continue to sauté until mushrooms are golden brown about 10–12 minutes.
3. In a large bowl, whisk together the eggs, half and half, chives, thyme, salt, and pepper. Place the goat cheese over the mushroom mixture and pour the egg mixture over the top.
4. Stir the mixture in the pan and cook over medium heat until the edges are set, but the center is still loose about 8–10 minutes.
5. Put the pan in the oven and finish cooking for an additional 8–10 minutes or until set. Allow cooling completely before slicing.

NUTRITION: Calories: 243 Carbohydrates: 5g Fat: 17g Protein: 15g

Mediterranean Frittata

Preparation time: 8 minutes.
Level: Easy.
Cooking time: 6 minutes.
Servings: 4
INGREDIENTS:

- 2 teaspoons of olive oil
- 3/4 cup of baby spinach, packed
- 2 green onions
- 4 egg whites, large
- 6 large eggs
- 1/3 cup of crumbled feta cheese, (1.3 ounces) along with sun-dried tomatoes and basil
- 2 teaspoons of salt-free Greek seasoning
- 1/4 teaspoon of salt

DIRECTIONS:

1. Take a boiler and preheat it. Take a ten-inch oven-proof skillet and pour the oil into it and keep the skillet on a medium flame.
2. While the oil gets heated, chop the spinach roughly and onions. Put the eggs, egg whites, Greek seasoning, cheese, as well as salt in a large mixing bowl and mix it thoroughly using a whisker.
3. Add the chopped spinach and onions into the mixing bowl and stir it well.
4. Pour the mixture into the pan and cook it for 2 minutes or more until the edges of the mixture set well.
5. Lift the edges of the mixture gently and tilt the pan so that the uncooked portion can get underneath it. Cook for another two minutes so that the whole mixture gets cooked properly.
6. Broil for two to three minutes till the center gets set. Your Frittata is now ready. Serve it hot by cutting it into four wedges.

NUTRITION: Calories: 178 Protein: 16g Fat: 12g Carbs: 2.2g

Savory Quinoa Egg Muffins with Spinach

Preparation time: 15 minutes.
Level: Average.
Cooking time: 20 minutes.
Servings: 4
INGREDIENTS:

- 1 cup of quinoa
- 2 cups of water/vegetable broth
- 4 ounces of spinach, which is about one cup
- 1/2 chopped onion
- 2 whole eggs
- 1/4 cup of grated cheese
- 1/2 teaspoon of oregano or thyme
- 1/2 teaspoon of garlic powder
- 1/2 teaspoon of salt

DIRECTIONS:

1. Take a medium saucepan and put water in it. Add the quinoa to the water and bring the whole thing to a simmer.
2. Cover the pan and cook it for 10 minutes till the water gets absorbed by the quinoa. Remove the saucepan from the heat and let it cool down.
3. Take a nonstick pan and heat the onions till they turn soft and then add spinach. Cook all of them together till the spinach gets a little wilted and then remove it from the heat.
4. Preheat the oven to 176°C. Take a muffin pan and grease it lightly.
5. Take a large bowl and add the cooked quinoa along with the cooked onions, spinach, and add cheese, eggs, thyme or oregano, salt, garlic powder, pepper and mix them together.
6. Put a spoonful of the mixture into a muffin tin. Make sure it is ¼ of a cup. In the preheated pan, put it in the pan and bake it for around 20 minutes.

NUTRITION: Calories: 61 Protein: 4g Fat: 3g Carbs: 6g

Spinach, Feta, and Egg Breakfast Quesadillas

Preparation time: 15 minutes.
Level: Easy.
Cooking time: 15 minutes.
Servings: 4
INGREDIENTS:

- 8 eggs (optional)
- 2 teaspoons olive oil
- 1 red bell pepper
- 1/2 red onion
- 1/4 cup milk
- 4 handfuls of spinach leaves
- 1 1/2 cup mozzarella cheese
- 5 sun-dried tomato tortillas
- 1/2 cup feta cheese
- 1/4 teaspoons salt
- 1/4 teaspoons pepper
- Spray oil

DIRECTIONS:

1. In a large non-stick pan over medium heat, add the olive oil. Once heated, add the bell pepper and onion, cook for 4-5 minutes until soft.
2. In the meantime, whisk together the eggs, milk, salt, and pepper in a bowl. Add in the egg/milk mixture into the pan with peppers and onions, stirring frequently, until eggs are almost cooked through.
3. Add in the spinach and feta, fold into the eggs, stirring until spinach is wilted and eggs are cooked through. Remove the eggs from heat and plate.
4. Spray a separate large non-stick pan with spray oil, and place over medium heat. Add the tortilla, on one half of the tortilla, spread about ½ cup of the egg mixture.
5. Top the eggs with around 1/3 cup of shredded mozzarella cheese. Fold the second half of the tortilla over, then cook for 2 minutes, or until golden brown.
6. Flip and cook for another minute until golden brown. Allow the quesadilla to cool completely, divide among the container, store for 2 days or wrap in plastic wrap and foil, and freeze for up to 2 months

NUTRITION: Calories: 213 Fat: 11g Carbs: 15g Protein: 15g

Mediterranean Feta and Quinoa Egg Muffins

Preparation time: 15 minutes.
Level: Easy.
Cooking time: 15 minutes.
Servings: 4
INGREDIENTS:

- 2 cups baby spinach finely chopped
- 1 cup chopped or sliced cherry tomatoes
- 1/2 cup finely chopped onion
- 1 tablespoon chopped fresh oregano
- 1 cup crumbled feta cheese
- 1/2 cup chopped (pitted) kalamata olives
- 2 teaspoons high oleic sunflower oil
- 1 cup cooked quinoa
- 8 eggs
- 1/4 teaspoon salt

DIRECTIONS:

1. Pre-heat oven to 350°F, and then prepare 12 silicone muffin holders on the baking sheet, or just grease a 12-cup muffin tin with oil and set aside.
2. Finely chop the vegetables and then heat the skillet to medium. After that, add the vegetable oil and onions and sauté for 2 minutes.
3. Then, add tomatoes and sauté for another minute, add spinach, and sauté until wilted for about 1 minute.
4. Place the beaten egg into a bowl and then add lots of vegetables like feta cheese, quinoa, veggie mixture as well as salt, and then stir well until everything is properly combined.
5. Pour the ready mixture into greased muffin tins or silicone cups, dividing the mixture equally. Then, bake it in an oven for 30 minutes or so.

NUTRITION: Calories: 113 Protein: 6g Fat: 7g Carbs: 5g

Chapter 11:
DESSERT RECIPES

Traditional Olive Oil Cake with Figs

Preparation time: 45 minutes.
Level: Easy.
Cooking time: 0 minutes.
Servings: 4
INGREDIENTS:

- 1/2-pound cooking apples, peeled, cored, and chopped
- 2 tablespoons fresh lemon juice
- 2 ½ cups all-purpose flour
- 1 teaspoon baking powder
- 1/4 teaspoon sea salt
- 1/2 teaspoon ground cinnamon
- A pinch of grated nutmeg
- 3/4 cup granulated sugar
- 1/2 cup extra-virgin olive oil
- 2 eggs
- 1/2 cup dried figs, chopped
- 2 tablespoons walnuts, chopped

DIRECTIONS
1. Begin by preheating your oven to 350ºF.
2. Toss the chopped apples with lemon juice and set them aside.
3. Then, thoroughly combine the flour, baking powder, sea salt, cinnamon, and nutmeg.
4. Then, beat the sugar and olive oil using your mixer at low speed.
5. Gradually fold in the eggs, one at a time, and continue to mix for a few minutes more until it has thickened.
6. Add the wet mixture to the dry ingredients and stir until you get a thick batter. Fold in the figs and walnuts and stir to combine well.
7. Spoon the batter into a parchment-lined baking pan and level the top using a wooden spoon.
8. Bake in the preheated oven for about 40 minutes, or until the tester comes out dry and clean. Let it cool on a wire rack before slicing and serving. Bon appétit!

NUTRITION: Calories: 339 Fat: 15.6g Carbs: 44.7g Protein: 6.4g

Mascarpone and Fig Crostini

Preparation time: 10 minutes.
Level: Easy.
Cooking time: 10 minutes.
Servings: 4
INGREDIENTS:

- 1 long French baguette
- 4 tablespoons (½ stick) salted butter, melted
- 1 (8-ounce) tub mascarpone cheese
- 1 (12-ounce) jar fig jam or preserves

DIRECTIONS:

1. Preheat the oven to 350°F. Slice the bread into ¼-inch-thick slices. Layout the sliced bread on a single baking sheet and brush each slice with the melted butter.
2. Put the single baking sheet in the oven and toast the bread for 5 to 7 minutes, just until golden brown.
3. Let the bread cool slightly. Spread about 1 teaspoon or so of the mascarpone cheese on each piece of bread. Top with 1 teaspoon of jam. Serve immediately.

NUTRITION: Calories: 445 Fat: 24g Carbs: 48g Protein: 3g

Traditional Mediterranean Lokum

Preparation time: 25 minutes.
Level: Easy.
Cooking time: 0 minutes.
Servings: 4
INGREDIENTS

- 1-ounce confectioners' sugar
- 3(½) ounces cornstarch
- 20 ounces caster sugar
- 4 ounces pomegranate juice
- 16 ounces cold water
- 3 tablespoons gelatin, powdered

DIRECTIONS

1. Line a baking sheet with parchment paper.
2. Mix the confectioners' sugar and 2 ounces of cornstarch until well combined.
3. In a saucepan, heat the caster sugar, pomegranate juice, and water over low heat.
4. In a mixing bowl, combine 4 ounces of cold water with the remaining cornstarch. Stir the mixture into the sugar syrup.
5. Slowly and gradually, add in the powdered gelatin and whisk until smooth and uniform.
6. Bring the mixture to a boil, turn the heat to medium and continue to cook for another 18 minutes, whisking constantly, until the mixture has thickened.
7. Scrape the mixture into the baking sheet and allow it to set in your refrigerator.
8. Cut your Lokum into cubes and coat with the confectioners' sugar mixture. Bon appétit!

NUTRITION: Calories: 208 Fat: 0.5g Carbs: 54.4g Protein: 0.2g

Chapter 12:

21 Days Meal Plan

21 DAYS		BREAKFAST		LUNCH		DINNER
o Day 1	o	Italian Breakfast Sausage with Baby Potatoes and Vegetables	o	Saffron Chicken Thighs and Green Beans	o	Garden Vegetable Stew
o Day 2	o	Cauliflower Fritters with Hummus	o	Bold Chorizo Paella	o	Lemon and Egg Soup
o Day 3	o	Overnight Berry Chia Oats	o	Moist Shredded Beef	o	Roasted Vegetable Soup
o Day 4	o	Raspberry Vanilla Smoothie	o	Hearty Beef Ragu	o	Mediterranean Tomato Soup
o Day 5	o	Blueberry Banana Protein Smoothie	o	Dill Beef Brisket	o	Tomato and Cabbage Puree Soup
o Day 6	o	Chocolate Banana Smoothie	o	Tasty Beef Stew	o	Athenian Avgolemono Sour Soup
o Day 7	o	Moroccan Avocado Smoothie	o	Meatloaf	o	Italian Bean Soup
o Day 8	o	Greek Yogurt with Fresh Berries, Honey and Nuts	o	Roasted Halibut with Banana Relish	o	Cucumber-Basil Salsa on Halibut Pouches
o Day 9	o	Greek Beans Tortillas	o	Scallops in Wine 'n Olive Oil	o	Dijon Mustard and Lime Marinated Shrimp
o Day 10	o	Bacon, Spinach and Tomato Sandwich	o	Seafood Stew Cioppino	o	Dill Relish on White Sea Bass
o Day 11	o	Coriander Mushroom Salad	o	Simple Cod Piccata	o	Garlic Roasted Shrimp with Zucchini Pasta
o Day 12	o	Cinnamon Apple and Lentils Porridge	o	Smoked Trout Tartine	o	Easy Seafood French Stew
o Day 13	o	Seeds and Lentils Oats	o	Tasty Tuna Scaloppine	o	Fresh and No-Cook Oysters
o Day 14	o	Orzo and Veggie Bowls	o	Thyme and Lemon on Baked Salmon	o	Easy Broiled Lobster Tails
o Day 15	o	Lemon Peas Quinoa Mix	o	Vegetarian Chili with Avocado Cream	o	Pork Tenderloin with Apple-Tarragon Sauce
o Day 16	o	Walnuts Yogurt Mix	o	Eggs with Zucchini Noodles	o	Miso-Garlic Pork Chops
o Day 17	o	Stuffed Pita Breads	o	Roasted Root Veggies	o	Slow Cooker Honey Mustard Pork with Pears
o Day 18	o	Farro Salad	o	Rustic Vegetable and Brown Rice Bowl	o	Slow Cooker Cranberry Pork Chops
o Day 19	o	Cranberry and Dates Squares	o	Roasted Brussels Sprouts and Pecans	o	Chicken and Olives
o Day 20	o	Mediterranean Egg Muffins with Ham	o	Roasted Vegetables and Zucchini Pasta	o	Chicken Bake
o Day 21	o	Sun-Dried Tomatoes, Dill, and Feta Omelet Casserole	o	Sautéed Collard Greens	o	Chicken and Artichokes

CONCLUSION

The Mediterranean is a prominent place. Dozens of different cultures and languages and cuisines blend, but this and its lush climate are part of the reason it's such a culinary powerhouse today. It's a bounty for both the soul and the body, fit for a peasant or an emperor. Hopefully, this carried you to wherever you wanted to be—whether that was health, performance, or simple curiosity.

This cookbook was not intended to be the be-all-end-all publication on Mediterranean food. Still, it was structured to serve as a knowledge basis—to give you a complete idea of the most basic of where to look when making choices for yourself. Just the essentials and then enough to get you started, with enough to carry you in confidence. We also tried to give you a reliable, calorie-precise guide to what you'll be eating, not so you can obsessively track every calorie, but so you can start thinking about the food choices you make every day hoping it will encourage you to find your way to a healthy lifestyle.

Changing your diet isn't a simple thing, but hopefully, we'll provide enough examples to inspire you on a culinary journey. Cooking and eating are a fundamental part of existence, and it is also one of the most rewarding for the body and spirit.

We emphasize how the Mediterranean diet and slow cookers can be a beautiful combination if you want to try a healthier version of your food. However, once you get used to the genuine taste that great food can deliver through a slow cooker, you will quickly adjust your schedule.

Quicker and faster is not always better, especially when it comes to instant food or fast foods, which is unhealthy, as we have seen in an overweight society, and harnesses several ailments. This was designed to learn the basics and assets that slow cooking can bring to your life with a bit of a twist on Mediterranean cuisine. You will find that there is no extra burden of time placed upon your schedule but a simple rearrangement of habit.

Once you have this new form of cooking blended into your routine, several cookbooks are designed for specific weight-loss diets, diabetic slow cooking, or even going Vegetarian. You will find yourself switching to healthier foods, saving on groceries, and using less energy.

The slow cooker can be an essential part of your life when you realize the multiple advantages of cooking healthy meals. Keep this cookbook handy and learn why slow cooker cooking is making such a famous comeback. You will discover that the slow cooker has always been a valuable tool, but perhaps, a little ahead of its time, for being noticed and appreciated.

But there's more to it. As you now know, the Mediterranean Diet is a lifestyle.

Not only you will lose weight because you're eating wholesome foods, exercising and managing stress will also contribute to the fat melting away. You can imagine that this won't happen overnight. You will have to make a conscious decision to choose what goes into your mouth and how you look after your body and mind in other ways.

At the very least, we have enriched your life most slightly. Enjoy your Mediterranean meals with your friends and family to the best effect. Whatever you've gleaned from this cookbook, the one thing we must say is Bon appétit!

INDEX OF RECIPES

Printed in Great Britain
by Amazon